THE COST OF LIVING IN NEW YORK CITY, 1926

THE COST OF LIVING IN NEW YORK CITY, 1926

NATIONAL INDUSTRIAL CONFERENCE BOARD, Inc.
NEW YORK
1926

Published, October, 1926
116

FOREWORD

QUESTIONS regarding living costs are constantly being raised. While such questions are often general in character, their answers must be specific if they are to be of value. They must take into account time and place, social and economic level, occupation and race, as well as number, age and sex of the members of the family group, type of living arrangement of the single man or the single woman, and the standard of living itself. All these are factors influencing the final determination. Moreover, the answers may be expressed either in terms of actual expenditures for living or of what would have to be spent, at current prices, to maintain an indicated standard of living. Information regarding what families are actually spending to live and the amounts they spend for specific items throws light on the problems of consumption. Information regarding the prices of a list of specified goods and services designed to represent a given level of consumption shows the cost of maintaining a definite standard of living.

Aside from its publications at various periods dealing with index numbers of the cost of living in the United States, of family budgets of American wage earners, and of correlated subjects, the National Industrial Conference Board has already issued eight reports on the actual cost of living among wage earners in representative industrial centers in the United States. In each of these localities an attempt was made to establish the minimum cost of maintaining a fair American standard of living among industrial workers, according to the means locally available for realizing that standard.

The present investigation attempts to determine the minimum cost of maintaining a fair American standard of living in New York City. Although studies of the cost of living in New York City have been made in the past by others, these have for the most part related to conditions in Manhattan

Borough, exclusively, and sometimes to only a small area thereof, or have concerned themselves with a limited type of family. The territory to be covered is so vast and the varieties of racial, occupational and economic levels are so numerous that no one, heretofore, has attempted to include all five boroughs in a cost of living survey, and no investigation since the post-war readjustment period has attempted a detailed analysis of prices which would take into account the various social and economic factors influencing the cost of living as a whole. The present investigation covers the entire city and is based on a large variety of living conditions. It considers the requirements of—(a) three types of families; (b) single men; (c) single women, in industrial occupations and in office employments. It should be a distinct contribution to the growing literature on the methods and results of retail price surveys.

The National Industrial Conference Board is under great obligation to the hundreds of retail dealers, realtors, organization executives and many others from whom pertinent data were secured and without whose cooperation such a survey could not readily have been made. The Board wishes to express to all these its appreciation for the assistance rendered.

This volume is the result of an investigation conducted by Miss M. L. Stecker and assistants, of the Conference Board's Research Staff, under the supervision of the Board's Staff Economic Council.

In the preparation of its studies the National Industrial Conference Board avails itself of the experience and judgment of the business executives who compose its membership and of recognized authorities in special fields, in addition to the scientific knowledge and equipment of its Research Staff. The publications of the Board thus finally represent the result of scientific investigation and broad business experience, and the conclusions expressed therein are those of the Conference Board as a body.

CONTENTS

Part I. Basic Data

PAGE
Introduction . . . 1
New York City and Its People . . . 1
Method of Investigation . . . 5
Establishing Standards . . . 6
Neighborhoods Visited . . . 9
Collecting Prices . . . 13
The Final Estimate . . . 14

CHAPTER
I. Housing . . . 15
Old vs. New Tenants . . . 15
Housing Shortage . . . 15
Rent Increases . . . 17
Effects of High Rents . . . 18
Smaller Living Quarters . . . 18
Increase in Home Ownership . . . 18
Housing Standards . . . 22
Sources of Rent Data . . . 25
Rents in the Bronx . . . 25
Rents in Brooklyn . . . 27
Rents in Manhattan . . . 29
Rents in Queens . . . 30
Rents in Richmond . . . 32
Summary . . . 35
II. Fuel and Light . . . 37
Coal, Gas, Kerosene . . . 37
Electricity . . . 40
Summary . . . 42
III. Food . . . 44
Minimum Food Requirements . . . 44
Price Data . . . 45
Quantity Data . . . 45
Summary . . . 50
IV. Clothing . . . 51
The Standard of Dress . . . 51
Minimum Clothing Requirements . . . 52
Price Data . . . 54
Summary . . . 59

CHAPTER PAGE
V. Sundries 60
Transportation 60
Recreation 64
Reading Material, Stationery, Postage, Telephone, etc. 64
Medical Care and Sick Benefits 65
Insurance 66
Organizations 67
Church, Charity and Gifts 68
Candy, Tobacco, etc. 68
Cleaning Supplies and Toilet Requisites 68
Furniture and Furnishings 68
Summary 69

Part II. The Cost of Living of Industrial Workers

VI. Cost of Living for Families 73
Housing 73
Fuel and Light 75
Food 76
Clothing 77
Sundries 84
The Complete Budget 85
VII. Cost of Living for Single Persons 89
Single Male Worker 89
Lodging 90
Food 90
Clothing 90
Sundries 91
The Complete Budget 91
Single Female Worker 93
Home Expenses 94
Clothing 96
Sundries 96
The Complete Budget 98

Part III. The Cost of Living of Office Workers

VIII. Cost of Living for Families 101
Housing 101
Fuel and Light 103
Food 103
Clothing 105
Sundries 111
The Complete Budget 111

CHAPTER PAGE
IX. Cost of Living for Single Persons 117
Lodging 117
Food 118
Clothing 121
Sundries 121
The Complete Budget 124
X. The Cost of Living in New York City 125
Industrial Workers 125
Office Workers 126
Summary 127

LIST OF TABLES

TABLE PAGE

1. Number of Residences in New York City, by Separate Boroughs and Kinds of Housing 20
2. Representative Minimum Range and Representative Average Minimum Rent per Room per Month for Specified Types of Housing in New York City, 1926 . . 34
3. Average Minimum Cost of Coal, Kerosene, Gas and Electricity per Year for Houses and Apartments of Different Sizes and Different Types in New York City, 1926 . 43
4. Minimum Requirements and Average Minimum Cost of Food for One Week, Based on the Needs of Two Men, Two Women, and One Older Child Under 14 Years of Age, or Two Younger Children, Living at a Fair American Standard in New York City, 1926 48
5. Average Minimum Retail Prices of Selected Articles of Wearing Apparel, Yard Goods, Clothing Accessories and Services in New York City, 1926 56
6. Average Minimum Cost of Transportation from Typical Residential Sections of New York City to Specified Business Centers of the Separate Boroughs, 1926 . 62
7. Average Minimum Outlay Necessary for Housing for One Month and for One Year for the Family of an Industrial Worker Living at a Fair American Standard in New York City, 1926 75
8. Average Minimum Cost of Fuel and Light for One Year for the Family of an Industrial Worker Living at a Fair American Standard in New York City, 1926 . . 76
9. Average Minimum Cost of Food for One Week and for One Year for the Family of an Industrial Worker Living at a Fair American Standard in New York City, 1926 77

10a. Average Minimum Cost of Clothing for One Year for a Married Male Industrial Worker Living at a Fair American Standard in New York City, 1926 . . 78

10b. Average Minimum Cost of Clothing for One Year for the Wife of an Industrial Worker Living at a Fair American Standard in New York City, 1926 . . 79

10c. Average Minimum Cost of Clothing for One Year for the 12-Year-Old Son of an Industrial Worker Living at a Fair American Standard in New York City, 1926 . . 80

TABLE PAGE

10d. Average Minimum Cost of Clothing for One Year for the 8-Year-Old Daughter of an Industrial Worker Living at a Fair American Standard in New York City, 1926 81
10e. Average Minimum Cost of Clothing for One Year for the 2-Year-Old Son of an Industrial Worker Living at a Fair American Standard in New York City, 1926 82
11. Average Minimum Cost of Clothing for One Year for the Family of an Industrial Worker Living at a Fair American Standard in New York City, 1926 83
12. Average Minimum Cost of Sundries for the Family of an Industrial Worker Living at a Fair American Standard in New York City, 1926 84
13. Average Minimum Cost of Maintaining a Fair American Standard of Living for the Family of an Industrial Worker in New York City, 1926. 87
14. Average Minimum Cost of Maintaining a Fair American Standard of Living for a Single Male Industrial Worker Living Apart from a Family Group in New York City, 1926 92
15. Average Minimum Cost of Clothing for One Year for a Single Female Industrial Worker Living at a Fair American Standard in New York City, 1926 . . 95
16. Average Minimum Cost of Maintaining a Fair American Standard of Living for a Single Female Industrial Worker Living as Part of a Family Group in New York City, 1926 97
17. Average Minimum Outlay Necessary for Housing for One Month and for One Year for the Family of an Office Worker Living at a Fair American Standard in New York City, 1926 102
18. Average Minimum Cost of Fuel and Light for One Year for the Family of an Office Worker Living at a Fair American Standard in New York City, 1926 . . 103
19. Average Minimum Cost of Food for One Week and for One Year for the Family of an Office Worker Living at a Fair American Standard in New York City, 1926 105
20a. Average Minimum Cost of Clothing for One Year for a Married Male Office Worker Living at a Fair American Standard in New York City, 1926 106
20b. Average Minimum Cost of Clothing for One Year for the Wife of an Office Worker Living at a Fair American Standard in New York City, 1926 107

TABLE PAGE

20c. Average Minimum Cost of Clothing for One Year for the 12-Year-Old Son of an Office Worker Living at a Fair American Standard in New York City, 1926 . . . 108

20d. Average Minimum Cost of Clothing for One Year for the 8-Year-Old Daughter of an Office Worker Living at a Fair American Standard in New York City, 1926 109

20e. Average Minimum Cost of Clothing for One Year for the 2-Year-Old Son of an Office Worker Living at a Fair American Standard in New York City, 1926 110

21. Average Minimum Cost of Clothing for One Year for the Family of an Office Worker Living at a Fair American Standard in New York City, 1926 111

22. Average Minimum Cost of Sundries for the Family of an Office Worker Living at a Fair American Standard in New York City, 1926 111

23. Average Minimum Cost of Maintaining a Fair American Standard of Living for the Family of an Office Worker in New York City, 1926 114

24. Average Minimum Cost of Clothing for One Year for a Single Female Office Worker Living at a Fair American Standard in New York City, 1926 120

25. Average Minimum Cost of Maintaining a Fair American Standard of Living for a Single Male Office Worker Living Apart from a Family Group in New York City, 1926 122

26. Average Minimum Cost of Maintaining a Fair American Standard of Living for a Single Female Office Worker Living Apart from a Family Group in New York City, 1926 123

27. Average Minimum Cost of Maintaining a Fair American Standard of Living for Industrial Workers in New York City, 1926 126

28. Average Minimum Cost of Maintaining a Fair American Standard of Living for Office Workers in New York City, 1926 127

LIST OF CHARTS

CHART PAGE

Map of New York City and Adjacent Territory....*Facing* 1

1. Average Minimum Cost per Week of Maintaining a Fair American Standard of Living for the Family of An Industrial Worker in New York City, 1926 . . . 72

2. Average Minimum Cost per Week of Maintaining a Fair American Standard of Living for the Family of An Office Worker in New York City, 1926 100

PART I: BASIC DATA

New York City and Adjacent Territory

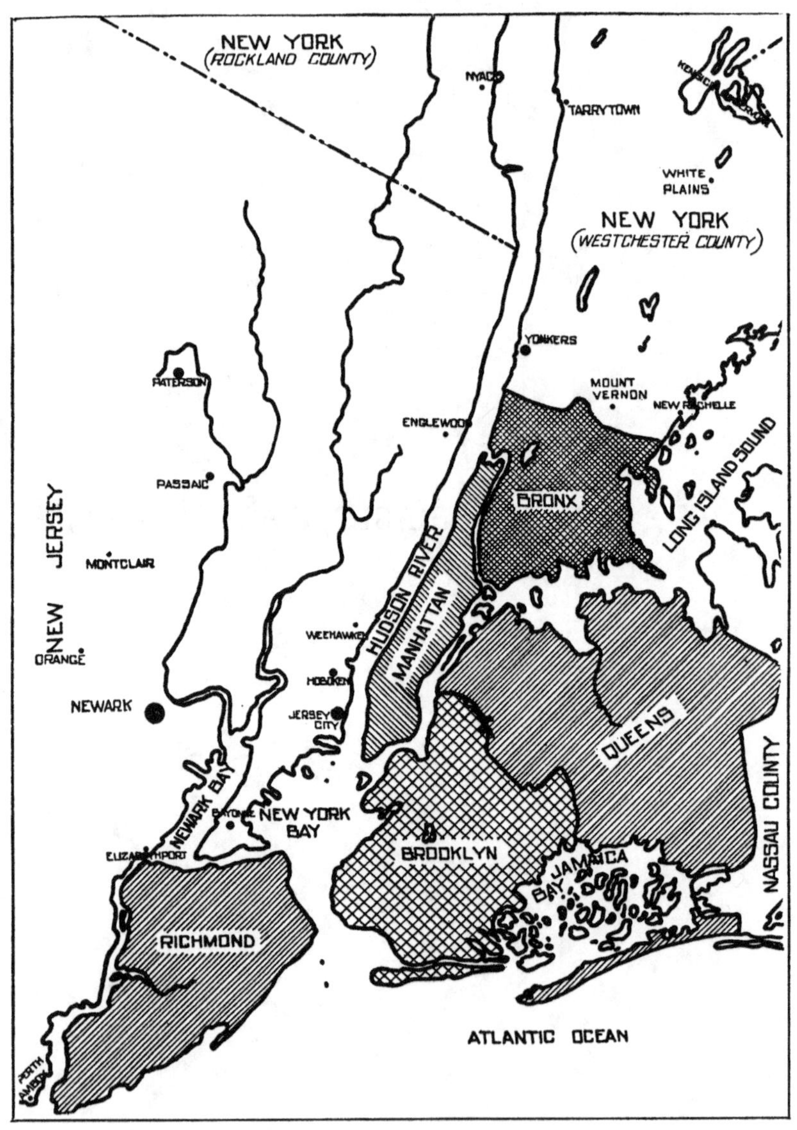

THE COST OF LIVING IN NEW YORK CITY, 1926

INTRODUCTION

THIS investigation of the cost of living was undertaken to ascertain the minimum cost of maintaining a fair American standard of living in New York City. An attempt was made to portray living conditions of (1) industrial workers and (2) office workers, and prices in the spring of 1926. The cost of living measured was related to the requirements of (1) a family group; (2) a single man without dependents; (3) a single woman without dependents. The investigation was designed to determine as far as possible the prevailing cost of living at the standard specified. The results are based on a survey of prices necessary to maintain this standard, and not on sums actually paid out by families.

New York City and Its People

The city of New York is composed of five separate boroughs, each of which, in turn, is a county of New York State. The present organization was effected in 1898, when the cities, towns and villages in the counties of New York, Kings, Queens, Richmond, and part of southern Westchester were consolidated. The two largest and most highly developed of these places were New York City, now the borough of Manhattan, and Brooklyn. Scattered settlements in farming areas, numerous suburban, and a few industrial, centers characterized the other boroughs. With the building of the first subways to the Bronx in 1904, that borough began to grow, especially as a residential area; fifteen years later many parts of Queens and more remote sections of Brooklyn were similarly brought into quicker and cheaper communication with the older centers and their population has increased and their business life has developed. Richmond, popularly known as Staten Island, is still without quick transportation to the other boroughs and can be reached from them only by a twenty-minute ferry ride across New York Bay. A number of important industries have, however, grown up in Richmond itself, which with plants in Perth Amboy, Bayonne and Elizabethport employ the bulk of the industrial workers on the island. Most of the commuters to Manhattan and Brooklyn work in the downtown offices.

The city of New York covers an area of 299 square miles, of which 41 are in the Bronx, 71 in Brooklyn, 22 in Manhattan, 108 in Queens and 57 in Richmond. The city extends 36 linear miles from the northern boundary of the Bronx to the southern boundary of Richmond, 16½ miles from Manhattan at the Hudson River to the eastern boundary of Queens, and 25 miles from the western limit of Richmond to the eastern limit of Queens.

The population of the city is still highly concentrated in the older boroughs, although in recent years movement from Manhattan and older sections of Brooklyn to the less densely settled areas has followed the route of the 5-cent carfare. The loss in the resident population of Manhattan is clearly shown in the table which follows—a loss of about 18% in six years. The non-resident population which flows in and out of Manhattan, however, more than makes up for this loss. On a typical business day upwards of three million persons are estimated to enter and leave the section of Manhattan south of 59th Street.[1] The table below gives the distribution of the area and the population of the city of New York. By comparing these figures one with another and with those for the state and the country as a whole, a fair idea may be ob-

Locality	Population		Land Area, Square Miles	Population Per Square Mile, 1926
	1920	1926 (estimated)		
United States	105,710,620	117,135,817	2,973,774	39.4
New York State	10,385,227	11,303,296	47,654	237.2
New York City	5,620,048	5,924,000	299	19,812.7
Bronx	732,016	900,000	41	21,951.2
Brooklyn	2,018,356	2,240,000	71	31,549.3
Manhattan	2,284,103	1,877,000	22	85,318.2
Queens	469,042	764,000	108	7,074.1
Richmond	116,531	143,000	57	2,508.8

[1] Harold M. Lewis, "The Transit and Transportation Problem," Regional Plan of New York and Its Environs, Engineering Series, Monograph Number Two, New York, 1926, p. 39.

tained of the layout of the city and the distribution of its population.

Thus, Queens has 36.1% of the area but only 12.9% of the population, and has next to the lowest density of population of any of the boroughs. Brooklyn has 23.7% of the area and 37.8% of the population; Richmond, with 19.1% of the area, has only 2.4% of the population; the Bronx has 13.7% of the area and 15.2% of the population; Manhattan, with only 7.4% of the area, has 31.7% of the population and thus the greatest concentration of population anywhere in the city, in fact, in the entire United States.

The population of New York City is probably the most cosmopolitan in the world. Totalling 5,620,048 in 1920 (estimated at 5,924,000 as of July 1, 1926), 20.7% were native white of native parentage; 33.3% were native white of foreign parentage; 7.7% were native white of mixed parentage; 35.4% were foreign born white. There were over 150,000 negroes, over 5,000 Chinese and over 2,000 Japanese. Of the approximately two million foreign born in the city, the largest proportion, 24%, came from Russia and Lithuania; the next largest, 19.3%, from Italy; 10%, from Ireland; 9.6%, from Germany; 7.2%, from Poland; 6.2%, from Austria.[1] Among the two and a third million of foreign or mixed parentage, there were 426,477 whose father or mother or both were born in Russia; 410,721 whose ancestors came from Italy; 404,838 from Ireland; 378,193 from Germany; 194,559 from Austria.[2] Every other country in the world is represented by greater or lesser numbers and some of them form quite distinct colonies in different sections of the city. Even among the native born, 12.5% were born outside of New York State[3] and thousands more within the state but outside the city of New York.

The population of New York City is more nearly in the prime of its working years than the average for the country as a whole. Practically 50% of the people in New York are between 20 and 50 years of age, as against 44% in the United States. The proportion is higher in Manhattan than

[1] United States, Bureau of the Census, Fourteenth Census of the United States, 1920, Vol. II, pp. 47; 49; 747.

[2] *Ibid.*, p. 941.

[3] *Ibid.*, p. 663.

in any of the other boroughs, but in all of them it is greater than the average for the entire country.[1] Among the gainfully occupied, 10 years of age and over, whose age was known, the distribution in 1920 was as follows:[2]

Total Population Ten Years of Age and Over Gainfully Employed	*Males* 1,837,196	*Females* 691,083
10–13 years of age	0.03%	0.06%
14 years of age	0.17	0.30
15 years of age	0.80	1.68
16 years of age	1.56	4.03
17 years of age	1.90	4.95
18 and 19 years of age	4.17	10.60
20 to 24 years of age	12.79	24.06
25 to 44 years of age	52.67	41.85
45 and over	25.91	12.49

The following proportions in each specified age group were gainfully employed in New York City in 1920:[3]

All Ages Ten Years and Over	*Males* 81.8%	*Females* 30.4%
14 years of age	6.9	4.5
15 years of age	34.1	27.0
16 years of age	65.1	58.6
17 years of age	78.8	73.8
18 and 19 years of age	86.9	75.0
20 to 24 years of age	94.1	56.2
25 to 44 years of age	98.1	29.3
45 to 64 years of age	93.4	19.8

The occupational diversification of New York City is notable, as well as the tremendous concentration in certain lines of employment. In 1920 the gainfully employed population of New York was distributed as follows:[4]

Occupation	Male		Female	
	Numbers	Per cent	Numbers	Per cent
Manufacturing and Mechanical Industries	748,183	40.7	204,129	29.5
Clerical Occupations	217,816	11.8	184,598	26.7
Trade	338,298	18.4	54,099	7.8
Domestic and Personal Service	149,623	8.1	156,667	22.7
Transportation	218,368	11.9	23,010	3.3
Professional Service	100,028	5.4	68,009	9.8
Public Service	60,030	3.3	845	.1
Agriculture, Forestry and Animal Husbandry	6,764	.4	345	.1
Extraction of Minerals	575	[a]	25	[a]
All Occupations	1,839,685	100.0	691,727	100.0

[a] Less than one-tenth of one per cent.

[1] *Ibid.*, pp. 154, 295–300.

[2] *Ibid.*, Vol. IV, pp. 456–457.

[3] *Ibid.*, pp. 452–455.

[4] *Ibid.*, pp. 186–203.

Approximately one-quarter of the gainfully employed males were laborers and unskilled factory workers of all kinds. There were 137,283 clerks (not in stores); 114,671 retail dealers; 91,625 salesmen; more than 88,000 semi-skilled factory operatives. Thirty-six other occupations each gave employment to more than 10,000 men and boys, the largest groups being 54,970 servants and waiters; 49,185 chauffeurs; 46,932 tailors; 42,664 machinists, millwrights and tool-makers; 42,478 carpenters; 42,449 bookkeepers, cashiers and accountants. Among the females, the largest numbers were laborers and unskilled factory workers—nearly 140,000; servants and waitresses, 94,658; stenographers and typists, 72,535; clerks (not in stores), 68,949; bookkeepers, cashiers and accountants, 40,234. Together, these five groups employed 60% of all women gainfully occupied in the city. Among the other 40%, semi-skilled factory operatives numbered nearly 32,000; saleswomen, 27,610; school teachers, 27,546; dressmakers and seamstresses (not in factories), 22,758; telephone operators, 20,068. Forty-nine other occupations gave employment to nearly 150,000 more.

Method of Investigation

Ascertaining the cost of living, even at the fair minimum American standard specified, for so heterogeneous a group, living in such diversified surroundings, was a task which presented several problems. To establish the standards, both as to articles to be priced and as to quantities required, and to determine where, in the 299 square mile area of the city, quotations should be secured, were as important as to collect the prices.

The very abundance of sources of information in itself was a complication, for they are practically innumerable. One of the most difficult problems throughout the survey has been what to eliminate, not because the data yielded would not have been useful but because limits were essential. The wholesale and retail trade, the banks, insurance and public utility companies, industrial establishments of all kinds, employing thousands of workers, have a wealth of experience, often in valuable record form, to be drawn on. There are about 2,000 social welfare organizations in the city, the great majority of which deal directly with the lives of working people, and whose judgment and opinion are of great value in such a connection. Much of this source material was used; much of it, equally valuable, of necessity had to be passed by. Enough was taken, however, to supply the background necessary for interpretation of the data obtained in the regular course of price collecting.

Establishing Standards

Estimates of the cost of living made up to this time have practically without exception started with the assumption that certain units or types were typical and that, even were adjustments to be made for other conditions, the starting point was fixed. These units have usually been, for a family, a group of five, consisting of the father and mother and three children under 14 years of age; for an individual, a single man or a single woman living apart from a family group and paying commercial rates for lodging, food, laundry, etc. These units are so at variance with the existing conditions,[1] however, that they have been entirely discarded in the present survey and an attempt has been made to set up a method of measuring the cost of living which is more nearly in conformity with reality.

All the evidence available, secured from industries and social welfare organizations alike, indicates that the typical working class family in New York City is one in which not only the father but the older boys and girls work and contribute to the family expenses. The Census shows that in the entire population of the city in 1920 there was an average of 1.2 children 14 years of age or under in a family group of 4.4 persons; which means 3.2 persons over 14 years of age per family.[2] The 1920 Census also shows that in this average family of 4.4 persons there was an average of 2 wage earners.[3] The New York State Commission of Housing and

[1] See, for example, Margaret Loomis Stecker, "Family Budgets and Wages," *American Economic Review*, September, 1921, pp. 447–465; Paul H. Douglas, "Is the Family of Five Typical?" *Journal of the American Statistical Association*, September, 1924, pp. 314–328.

[2] Fourteenth Census of the United States, Vol. II, pp. 295–300; 1268. By boroughs, the average size of family was: Bronx, 4.4; Brooklyn, 4.4; Manhattan, 4.3; Queens, 4.3; Richmond, 4.9.

[3] *Ibid.*, Vol. II, p. 1268; *ibid.*, Vol. IV, p. 128.

Regional Planning in 1924 estimated that in New York City each person with a separate income supported 1.08 dependents and that the annual income of each family was one and one-quarter times the individual income of main support.[1]

Such being the case, it is obvious that the expenditures for which the adult male head of the family is responsible, and which must be counted as his necessary cost of living, are less than in the hitherto accepted standard family. Not only has he fewer persons to provide for, but with other wage earners in the group contributing to the joint expenses their fair share of the pro-rated cost, the head of the family pays proportionately less of the charges which are fixed more or less regardless of the number provided for, or which actually decrease per capita the more members there are in the group. Conversely, if, as all the evidence indicates, the typical single woman wage earner in New York City, especially in industrial employments, is young and lives at home as part of the family group, her expenses are of a totally different character than are indicated by the needs of the hitherto accepted standard young woman paying commercial rates for the necessaries of life. On the other hand, the cost of living at commercial rates is an important factor in the lives of some minimum standard women workers in office employments in the city, relatively few though they be. The usual cost of living at home, even at the minimum standard, is apparently more often covered by a flat rate payment to the family in the case of single men than in the case of single women; and, again, far more minimum standard single men than single women are living independently of the family group.

The requirements established in the present investigation for measuring the minimum cost of maintaining a fair American standard of living for families of varying size and composition, for single men and for single women, were partly theoretical, and partly based on available data regarding consumption habits. No comprehensive survey has been made recently by the results of which either items or quantities might

[1] State of New York, Commission of Housing and Regional Planning, Report, Legislative Document (1924) No. 43, Albany, 1924, pp. 67–69.

be tested; observation and the opinions of dealers and others closely in touch with the lives of working people were used to supplement and bring up to date budgets constructed for earlier years.[1] Thus, for the family group unit, consisting of a man, woman and one or more children, the food requirements were worked out by taking the calories needed by persons of specified age, sex and occupation and combining them in different size groups. For housing, the usual standards of health, decency and safety were accepted and the number of rooms required was estimated for families of varying size and composition; for fuel and light, the quantities allowed were dependent on the number of rooms to be served; for clothing, budgets were constructed for a man, a woman and several children of different age and sex, based on reasonable variety and durability of the garments; for sundries, consideration of modest needs influenced the necessarily arbitrary allowances.

For the single man, the unit adopted was that of the unmarried worker living apart from a family group, or that of one paying a flat rate for his board and being entirely independent of the family. Requirements for room, board and laundry as well as for the services ordinarily performed by women in the home, and for sundries of various kinds required by a young man without a home in the city, were established. Data by which the cost of living as a contributing member in a family group might be estimated are also given. For the unmarried woman, the problem of standards was one of determining her fair share of the expenses of the family in which she lives. To take account, however, of the needs of the young woman who pays commercial rates for board, room and laundry, the cost of living for this type was also estimated, based on the facilities available for meeting these needs.

It is not claimed that these standards are exact, nor is it necessary that they should be so in a survey which is based largely on samples, and the results of which can be expressed

[1] See, for example, earlier reports by the National Industrial Conference Board on the cost of living among wage earners, *e. g.*, Research Reports Nos. 22, 24; Special Reports Nos. 7, 8, 13, 16, 19, 21.

only as averages. They are, however, believed to be logical and representative of balanced consumption requirements for maintaining a fair minimum American standard in New York City in 1926.

It should be remembered, however, that the exigencies of a cost of living survey do not permit that every possible condition be met in a budget. Even among persons of limited means, a greater variety of goods and services are used than could judiciously be priced in such an investigation. Thus it became necessary to select representatives of the different items, increasing the quantity allowed to make up for the consumption of other goods which were not included. In the matter of food, for example, 40 items were listed in the Board's budget; in practice, families undoubtedly buy many kinds of fruits, vegetables, meats and cereals in addition to those which were included, but obviously it would have been impracticable to price them all. So, also, in respect to clothing, recreation and other items involving matters of taste, it would have been impossible to meet all requirements. By drawing up a logical, well-balanced and broadly representative budget, however, such individual changes as are necessary can be made with little difficulty, since the cost estimated on the basis of the items included is adequate to meet the cost of a budget having greater variety.

Neighborhoods Visited

Having established the requirements for the maintenance of a fair minimum American standard of living, these were priced in different sections of the city. The selection of the districts in which prices were to be secured presented another problem. How choose, from an area of 299 square miles, inhabited by nearly six million people, shopping centers and residence districts which would present a fair cross-section? A few blocks in the Bronx, Brooklyn or Manhattan often contain as many people as the average size American city; one street of so-called neighborhood stores may supply the needs of a similar number of people. In 1922 it was estimated that there were nearly 95,000 retail outlets in the city, including over 28,000 grocery stores; 12,000 department stores; 7,000 clothing stores; 3,500 shoe stores; 4,000 furniture dealers, and others in like proportion.[1] There are large areas inhabited almost exclusively by negroes or by Italians or by Jews; there are settlements of people from Spain and Bohemia and from numerous other countries; there are neighborhoods distinctively German and those where the Irish element seems to predominate, and, of course, persons of native white stock everywhere.

The choice of localities to be surveyed for prices was finally made according to the following plan: Since it was proposed to picture a fair minimum American standard of living, it was considered that native born white residents were typical. Native born persons, however, may be of native, foreign or mixed parentage. The native born white population of New York City of foreign or mixed parentage is considerably greater than the native born of native parentage. Adding together native born of foreign and those of mixed parentage, it is found that they form the following percentages of the total white population: in the Bronx, 45%; in Brooklyn, 43.8%; in Manhattan, 39.6%; in Queens, 43.7%; in Richmond, 39.3%.[2]

It was, therefore, determined to adopt for purposes of this survey the native born of foreign parentage as most representative of American wage earners in New York City. The countries furnishing the largest numbers of native born of foreign or mixed parentage in New York City in 1920, as already noted, were Russia, Italy, Ireland, Germany. The first two of these racial groups were considered to be less suitable for the present purpose than the last two, because (1) most of the former probably are not old enough to meet the requirements of this study, the great tide of immigration from these countries having set in between 1890 and 1900, while the immigration from Germany and Ireland was of much earlier origin. The American born children of these earlier immigrants would account for a greater number of

[1] The Crowell Publishing Company, "National Markets and National Advertising," New York, 1923, p. 54.

[2] Fourteenth Census of the United States, Vol. II, p. 49.

American born industrial and office workers with families than the more recently arrived immigrants from Russia and Italy. (2) The traditions of the German and Irish immigrant stock are more nearly American than are those of immigrants from Italy or Russia, and so-called American standards would be likely to prevail more completely in the second generation of the former races than in the second generation of the latter. (3) Persons of Russian and Italian birth or descent are found in a relatively small variety of industrial and office employments as contrasted with those of German or Irish ancestry.

For these reasons, it was determined that neighborhoods in which native born white persons of German or Irish parentage live should constitute the localities in which data regarding the cost of living should be secured. To find where these sections of the city are, maps made by the New York City 1920 Census Committee were used.[1] The first of these gives the sanitary areas (40 acres) by nativity of parents; the second, by nativity of the foreign born. By assuming, quite fairly, it would appear, that the native born of foreign parentage live in the same general localities as the foreign born of the same parentage, it was possible to select sections of the city in which it might be said that the native born of German or Irish parentage predominate. It should be clearly understood, however, that few neighborhoods are exclusively inhabited by any one racial group, especially one whose standards conform closely to a generally prevailing pattern or type, and that in the areas chosen for study in the present investigation, many other nationalities than those specified as predominant were represented. The investigation is, therefore, far more than a study of the cost of living of persons of American birth and German or Irish parentage.

The rough boundaries of the neighborhoods in which the bulk of the price data were collected are as follows, together with the predominant racial stock of American birth.

[1]New York City Census Committee, Inc., "Statistical Sources of Demographic Studies of Greater New York, 1920," Supplementary Maps.

Borough	Definition of Area	Predominant Racial Stock of American Birth
Bronx		
	(1) Bedford Park Boulevard, Webster and Park Avenues, 176th Street, Jerome Avenue (West Bronx)	German; some from Russia and Hungary
	(2) Tremont Avenue, Eastern Boulevard, Lafayette and Rosedale Avenues (East Bronx)	German; a few from Italy
Brooklyn		
	(1) Sterling Place, Fourth Avenue, 23d Street, Greenwood Cemetery, Prospect Park West, Sixth Street, Eighth Avenue, Vanderbilt Avenue, Atlantic Avenue, Franklin Avenue, Eastern Parkway (Park Slope—Gowanus)	Irish
	(2) Flushing, Irving, Myrtle, Evergreen Avenues, Broadway (Bushwick)	German; some from Russia and Italy
	(3) Foster, Flatbush, Flatlands, Ocean Avenues (Flatlands)	German and Italian
Manhattan		
	(1) West 58th Street, Eighth Avenue, West 30th Street, Hudson River (San Juan Hill and Hell's Kitchen)	Irish
	(2) East River, East 79th Street, First Avenue, East 84th Street, Park Avenue, 98th Street, Third Avenue, East 94th Street, First Avenue, East 89th Street (Yorkville)	German; some from Ireland
	(3) 134th Street, Amsterdam Avenue, 146th Street, Hudson River; 155th Street, Amsterdam Avenue, 159th Street, St. Nicholas Avenue (Manhattanville and Lower Washington Heights)	German and Irish
Queens		
	(1) Northern Boulevard, 38th Avenue, 28th Street, 30th Avenue, 31st Street, Ditmars Avenue, Hazen Avenue (Long Island City and Astoria)	German; a few from Ireland and Italy
	(2) Jamaica	
	(3) Flushing	
Richmond		
	(1) Bay Street, Victory Boulevard, Clove Road, Vanderbilt Avenue (Stapleton)	German
	(2) District West of Amboy Road in neighborhood of Great Kills and Eltingville	German

As the investigation developed it appeared that in a few instances certain conditions necessary for a complete survey of the cost of living were not to be found in these areas and others were studied as required. For example, in Brooklyn, the Flatlands district in Flatbush originally chosen was found to be largely a new development of one and two family houses but this was included for housing because that particular type is an important feature of the present rent situation. The west side of Manhattan below 59th Street, which at the time of the 1920 Census was a populous Irish-American center had so changed with the exodus of large numbers of its population to the newer sections of Queens, and the rapid westward movement of the theatrical district above 42nd Street that it no longer retains its neighborhood character. Below 42nd Street, Irish-Americans are being replaced by Greeks, Turks, Armenians, Albanians and other southeastern peoples. The upper Manhattan sections, on the other hand, not originally included, were later surveyed for rents because they seemed to be most typical of the older apartment house neighborhoods. Neither of the districts originally selected in the Bronx contained many representatives of minimum conditions, since both are fairly new, and minimum housing for both the industrial and the office worker had to be found in older sections of the borough. In Richmond attention was concentrated on Stapleton because the other section originally chosen has a relatively small population distributed over a fairly large area. Port Richmond was visited, however, for certain data. In Queens, attention was centered on Long Island City, Astoria and Jamaica, although some prices were collected in Flushing. The areas covered for each item are noted in the pages which follow where the cost is under consideration.

Collecting Prices

Having determined the goods and services necessary to meet the minimum requirements of the families of industrial or office workers living at a fair American standard and having determined what sections of the city would best represent conditions under which these people live, agents of the National Industrial Conference Board went into these neighborhoods and collected prices of the goods and services thus specified. The field work alone covered a period of three months and more than a thousand persons, firms and organizations were consulted for price data and other facts and figures which would make possible an adequate interpretation.

After prices of the goods and services making up a fair minimum American standard of living were secured, in the neighborhoods selected on the basis previously described, these prices were averaged for each item. They are, therefore, not the very lowest figures which could be secured but are averages of the lowest prices charged in the various shops visited. As some stores were catering to a relatively high and some to a relatively less expensive standard of living, it appears that some of the prices collected were relatively high or relatively low in comparison with the general level. So far as can be seen, however, these balance up and the total, combined into a logical budget, gives a fair picture.

The Final Estimate

When the quantities of the different kinds of goods and services required to maintain a well-balanced minimum American standard of living had been estimated, these were multiplied by the averages of the prices secured for the respective items, to get the total cost of living. The results, while they cannot claim to be a complete picture of the cost of living in New York City, even at a fair minimum American standard, are believed to be a fair approximation of average minimum conditions and to tell as truly as average can, what the situation is. It should always be remembered, however, that the results are averages, representative of conditions in general but probably fitting few if any individual cases exactly.

CHAPTER I

HOUSING

Old vs. New Tenants

OF ALL the necessaries of life, that which bears most heavily on the family of small or moderate means in New York City is the cost of shelter. Traditionally a city of high rents, lack of building construction from 1917 onwards, the high price of building materials and labor, land booms and extensive speculative operations have so increased values within the last ten years that the outlay required for many kinds of housing has practically doubled. This is not so true for those families who have lived continuously in the same house or apartment, since the law of 1920, amended each year subsequently, limiting the increase in rents which might be charged has protected those who did not move.[1] Where families have been forced to change, however, and thus became new tenants, large increases in the outlay necessary for rent have often been required, while at the same time the price asked for the apartment thus vacated has been increased for the next tenant. An analysis of variations in rents by period of tenancy of 1,703 four-room apartments in October, 1923 showed that tenants who had lived in their apartments less than a year were paying, in the average, 55% more rent than tenants who had lived in the same apartment for five years.[2] Rents being paid in certain tenements, as revealed in the present investigation, showed a difference fully as great as this in the spring of 1926.

Housing Shortage

The shortage in housing which became most acute in 1920 and culminated in the law noted above, placing restrictions

[1] Laws of New York, 1920, ch. 136. There have been numerous amendments but the basic protection to the old tenant still holds.

[2] State of New York, Commission of Housing and Regional Planning, Report, Legislative Document (1925) No. 91, Albany, 1925, p. 26.

on rent increases, also served to bring into use once more apartments which, because of their age and general inferiority were unoccupied so long as better quarters were to be obtained for the rent which could be paid. As rents increased, however, less and less desirable quarters were all that were available for the customary outlay. While, therefore, in March, 1916, said to be a normal period, there were 6.52% vacancies in the old law tenements and 4.03% in the new law[1] or an average of 5.60%, in February, 1921, vacancies had been reduced to .16% in the old law houses and .15% in the new law houses, an average of only .15%.[2] Since 1921, vacancies have increased but they have been much more frequently found in the newer than in the older houses.

These vacancies are due not only to the much larger volume of construction of the higher priced apartments, but also to the fact, which applies to old and new houses alike, that the higher rents are driving families into smaller living quarters. Extensive building in the more suburban areas, moreover, is attracting many from more crowded older sections of the city, while decreased immigration is said to account for vacancies in the poorest houses.

The New York State Commission of Housing and Regional Planning reported in 1925 that of the 85,000 suites provided by new construction during the preceding year, 50,000 rented for upwards of $15 per room per month, and thus "are beyond the rent paying ability of two-thirds of the population."[3] "Commercial enterprises cannot build adequate apartments today to rent for less than $12.50 per room per month. The average family in old law houses cannot afford more than $7.00."[4] The Mayor's Committee on Housing reported early in 1924 "That the great majority of people

[1] So-called "old law tenements" are those built before the passage of the tenement house law of 1901; almost without exception they are below the standard established for new construction, and most of them cannot be brought up to this standard. Most of them have the same faults that were condemned in investigations made more than sixty years ago. *Ibid.*, pp. 16–17. "New law houses," built to conform to standards required by the laws of 1901, 1909 and 1921, meet certain minimum requirements as to light, ventilation, safety, sanitation, etc. New York State, Laws of 1901, ch. 334; Laws of 1909, ch. 99; Laws of 1921, ch. 218.

[2] New York State Commission of Housing and Regional Planning, Report, 1925, *op. cit.*, p. 17.

[3] *Ibid.*, p. 14.

[4] *Idem.*

adversely affected by high rents are the families of hundreds of thousands of the 'white collar' element . . . whose salary is below $2,000 per annum. . . . The habits and living conditions of this element impel them to live in the better neighborhoods and in a better class of house, most often in the new law tenement and it is exactly in these houses . . . where the question of high rent pinches and affects the occupants most."[1]

Rent Increases

At any standard of living the lowest cost housing is the oldest or least convenient as to layout or location. This is as true in the fashionable Park Avenue section of Manhattan as it is in the humblest working class neighborhoods. The top floor of walkups, old-fashioned heating or lighting or plumbing, inconvenient arrangement of rooms and dozens of other circumstances keep down the rents of older houses in competition with newer places supplying what the older ones lack. But rents of the older houses are low only relatively, and many types of older housing are in such great demand that they seldom come on the market for rent at all. The Federal Reserve Bank of New York reported that in October, 1925, rents of the cheaper houses were 90% above the level of 1914, while rents of apartments costing $15 to $30 per room in 1920 were only 60% higher.[2] The latter level represents a decrease of 9% from the peak of 1921, while rents of the cheaper places had gone down less than 1%. As yet, however, rents of the two are by no means identical and while at the present time there are several alternatives in housing available well above the minimum, minimum housing itself offers comparatively little range of choice.

Within the last year or two, with the increased quantity of new houses available there is everywhere found a disposition to come down in the established rent for this type of housing. In the high class apartments this takes the form of concessions of a month or more rent; in the less expensive

[1] Report of the Mayor's Committee on Housing, New York, February 29, 1924, pp. 13–14.

[2] *Monthly Review of Credit and Business Conditions*, Second Federal Reserve District, November, 1925, pp. 6–7.

places, if the tenant appears desirable, a few dollars a month may be taken off the price originally quoted. Among the popular older houses, such concessions are not found; indeed, tenants usually are waiting to seize any vacancy which may occur and there is little to rent. As yet there has been no break in rents at the lowest ranges so noticeable as to demand consideration.

Effects of High Rents

Smaller Living Quarters

Smaller living quarters provide one of the most frequent answers to the high rent problem. Whereas the average number of rooms occupied by families of moderate means formerly averaged four, the present average is three and a fraction.[1] Moreover, the practice of "doubling up" has so increased that it is not at all uncommon to find one door bell with several names on it and several families sharing a common kitchen and bath room. The latter method of meeting the high rent situation is particularly economical because, as a rule, the larger apartments rent for relatively less per room than do the smaller.

Increase in Home Ownership

Another result of the extremely high rents is the tremendous increase in home ownership within the last few years. New York, even in Queens and Richmond boroughs, has been traditionally a city of rented homes. According to the United States Census,[2] the following proportions prevailed at the last three Census periods:

Locality	Percent of All Homes—					
	Rented			Owned		
	1900	1910	1920	1900	1910	1920
United States	53.9	54.2	54.4	46.1	45.8	45.6
New York State	66.9	69.1	69.3	33.1	30.9	30.7
New York City	87.9	88.3	87.3	12.1	11.7	12.7
Bronx	80.4	86.9	91.8	19.6	13.1	8.2
Brooklyn	82.0	81.7	80.7	18.0	18.3	19.3
Manhattan	95.6	97.1	97.9	4.4	2.9	2.1
Queens	63.6	65.4	63.3	36.4	34.6	36.7
Richmond	63.3	62.3	57.3	36.7	37.7	42.7

[1] Report of the Mayor's Committee on Housing, *op. cit.*, p. 6. See, also, New York, State Commission of Housing and Regional Planning, Report, 1924, *op. cit.*, pp. 37, ff.

[2] Fourteenth Census of the United States, 1920, Vol. II., pp. 1284, 1288.

Exact data showing the change in home ownership within the last five years are not available. The existing numbers of one and two family houses give a fair indication of what has taken place, however, since few of the single family houses are for rent and in the two family dwellings the owner customarily occupies one floor, renting out the rest of the house. In Table 1 the number of different kinds of housing in the separate boroughs as reported for the year ending March 31 of each year since 1918 is shown.

This table indicates a tremendous increase in the number of one and two family houses within the last five years. Many of these buildings, especially the least expensive houses, are put up wholesale, so to speak. That is, a common design of layout, construction, materials, etc., is reproduced dozens, even hundreds, of times, with a possible alteration of roof shape or color, but with a similarity so complete as to make it difficult for the occupant to know his own home without some peculiar mark of identification. For block after block in the Bronx, Brooklyn and Queens, these houses have been going up and sold on easy payments to prospective occupants. One contractor in Flushing advertised the construction of two thousand such one family houses to be sold; others have put up hundreds of the one or two family type. Developments of this kind in the Bronx[1] and Brooklyn have been less extensive and for the most part are of a somewhat better class than much of the building in Queens and in addition to homes for owner occupancy, a good many places have been available to rent. In Manhattan, there has been practically no new building of working-class housing, and in Richmond there was little evidence of the wholesale building found in Queens, for example, but much to indicate a normal growth of more individual units.

Real estate operators quite generally credit the great increase in home ownership to high rents, as well as to the easy terms on which such dwellings may be bought, and to the fact that relatively little of the newer housing except of the more expensive type is for rent. High rents have been

[1] In the Bronx large areas have been developed by selling lots to individuals who have erected thereon their own houses. These sections contain a wide variety of housing.

TABLE 1: NUMBER OF RESIDENCES IN NEW YORK CITY, BY SEPARATE BOROUGHS AND KINDS OF HOUSING[a]

(New York City Department of Taxes and Assessments)

Type of Housing	1918	1919	1920	1921	1922	1923	1924	1925	1926
Bronx									
One family dwellings	15,238	13,612	13,412	13,602	14,303	15,988	17,049	18,553	19,667
Two family dwellings	9,706	8,680	8,669	8,776	9,034	8,773	10,812	12,382	13,595
Tenements without elevators	12,924	10,959	10,924	11,023	11,100	11,402	12,126	12,055	12,926
Hotels and elevator apartments	81	75	75	82	86	87	87	81	101
Total	37,949	33,326	33,080	33,483	34,523	37,250	40,074	43,071	46,289
Brooklyn									
One family dwellings	67,490	67,857	67,948	71,136	72,680	76,155	80,623	86,260	89,802
Two family dwellings	52,938	53,337	53,879	55,295	56,455	59,685	63,816	69,507	71,473
Tenements without elevators	48,693	48,744	48,750	49,155	49,824	50,331	51,523	54,435	55,524
Hotels and elevator apartments	287	286	285	282	279	295	330	358	373
Total	169,408	170,224	170,862	175,868	179,238	186,466	196,292	210,560	217,172
Manhattan									
One family dwellings	23,324	23,946	23,592	28,271	23,111	22,636	21,740	21,721	20,961
Two family dwellings	2,639	2,604	2,602	2,629	2,639	2,691	4,182	4,546	4,182
Tenements without elevators	40,403	40,263	40,423	39,789	39,649	39,157	38,435	37,501	36,882
Hotels and elevator apartments	2,335	2,337	2,299	2,341	2,375	2,406	2,525	2,648	2,763
Total	68,701	69,150	68,916	73,030	67,774	66,890	66,882	66,416	64,788

Queens									
One family dwellings	41,979	43,164	44,869	46,035	51,228	61,955	70,289	80,321	87,365
Two family dwellings	18,262	17,320	17,853	18,033	19,455	22,415	26,162	31,611	35,229
Tenements without elevators	5,483	6,476	6,527	6,668	6,748	6,919	6,989	7,220	7,871
Hotels and elevator apartments	214	209	209	215	219	212	139	147	142
Total	65,938	67,169	69,458	70,951	77,650	91,501	103,579	119,299	130,607
Richmond									
One family dwellings	16,775	16,801	17,538	18,606	19,944	21,840	23,114	24,447	26,435
Two family dwellings	2,283	2,398	2,464	2,611	2,725	2,952	3,585	3,955	4,257
Tenements without elevators	544	554	554	557	550	550	572	573	572
Hotels and elevator apartments	65	64	65	90	90	88	77	74	68
Total	19,667	19,817	20,621	21,864	23,309	25,430	27,348	29,049	31,332
New York City									
One family dwellings	164,806	165,380	167,359	177,650	181,266	198,574	212,815	231,302	244,230
Two family dwellings	85,828	84,339	85,467	87,344	90,308	97,516	108,557	122,001	128,736
Tenements without elevators	108,047	106,996	107,178	107,192	107,871	108,359	109,645	111,784	113,775
Hotels and elevator apartments	2,982	2,971	2,933	3,010	3,049	3,088	3,158	3,308	3,447
Total	361,663	359,686	362,937	375,196	382,494	407,537	434,175	468,395	490,188

[a] As reported for the year ending March 31 of each year.

a frequent theme in propaganda for the sale of dwellings for owner occupancy. According to the sales prospectuses, the outlay necessary for amortizing the mortgage, paying the interest, taxes and insurance on a brand new house with alluring modern devices is so little more than the rent paid for suites in old and inconvenient tenements as to attract thousands of wage earners who if they have a few hundred dollars in the bank to put down as the first payment, and a steady job, see possible the realization of their dreams to secure more modern conveniences. Policemen, firemen, letter carriers, mechanics and industrial workers have bought these houses.

While these new dwellings are being bought by people from all over the metropolitan district, there is a notable movement from the older sections of the city. Eighty-five per cent of one group of 300 houses put up by a contractor in Queens were bought by persons from Manhattan and the Bronx; another builder claims to advertise only in newspapers read largely by definite racial groups, formerly concentrated in the older boroughs.

The neediest classes of the population have as yet had little benefit from this new building, although in time it may serve to bring down the rents of the old housing which is being vacated. These classes include the minimum standard industrial workers who have no savings to invest in a home and whose earnings are insufficient to meet the payments; and the general average of moderate salaried office employees who may have the financial means of making the investment but who feel that the surroundings would not be congenial. The determination of the minimum cost of providing such housing as would meet the elementary physical and social necessities of these groups presented the most serious difficulty connected with the present study of the minimum cost of maintaining a fair American standard of living in New York City.

Housing Standards

The establishment of minimum housing standards under prevailing conditions is attended with extreme difficulty. Those adopted for this investigation are recognized as more or less arbitrary but have the virtue at least of not falling below accepted practice. Houses which were considered to be meeting the minimum standards for the family of an industrial worker, that is, a man engaged at manual labor, who wears overalls or other informal dress at his work and whose social and cultural tastes and opportunities are rather simple, were required to be in decent neighborhoods, were in at least a fair state of repair, cleanliness and sanitation, and had a bath room for the exclusive use of one family. Such housing was usually without central heat; sometimes there was hot water or electricity or both, sometimes there was not. For the so-called "white collar" worker, or office employee, central heat was added to the requirements, since houses in neighborhoods in which such families live usually contain these improvements. There might or might not be elevators or janitor service, parquet floors, panelled walls, side bracket lights, closets for ironing boards and kitchen waste containers and all the other features which go to make the new places socially desirable quite as much as they make them comfortable, and each of which seems to add a few dollars to the price charged, without any real addition to the fundamental requirements.

As already indicated, a choice of localities to be covered in a survey of the cost of living in New York City was required because of the tremendous area to be covered. The sections selected by the criteria already described proved without exception to meet the needs of this survey in one way or another, and while all were not covered for every purpose, all were surveyed for rents. Because, also, various types of housing were not to be located in the areas specified, these were studied where found. It is not claimed that every type of housing and every range of rents has been covered; without a complete census that would have been impossible. It is believed, however, that fair samples have been chosen and that the rents specified are representative of the class of housing with which this survey is concerned, namely, minimum American standards for industrial and office workers.

A comparison of rents in the separate boroughs, from the point of view of the cost of securing identical accommodations, is out of the question for all types of housing because the character of accommodations available differs greatly. In the two older boroughs, Manhattan and Brooklyn, the large, many family tenements[1] and smaller unit "railroad" apartments[2] provide practically the only minimum cost housing available for industrial workers. These are old, often without heat or hot water, electricity or bath rooms, except for a toilet in the hall or basement used by several families. In much housing of this minimum type, the law is complied with and that is all. Were the buildings to be torn down, they would not be replaced with space which could be rented for anything approaching the present rent.

In the newer boroughs, until the growth of industry and population which followed the development of cheap transportation, there were many scattered towns and villages which had been consolidated into the making of the city of New York, and here the older houses are single or double unit frame dwellings with only occasionally larger units. In the Bronx, some of these older structures have been cleared away for more modern houses, especially of the multiple unit type, although many smaller unit frame buildings are still found; in Queens and Richmond, where the pressure for land is relatively less acute, many of them remain and house those who can make only a minimum outlay for rent, or whose ownership of the premises ties them there.

For the better class of dwelling, also, a contrast in available accommodation exists. In Manhattan, the single unit frame house is now almost a curiosity, the great bulk of the people living in multiple unit dwellings; in the Bronx and Brooklyn, frame houses are rapidly disappearing in favor of the larger structures except in certain high class districts. In Queens and Richmond, on the other hand, single frame houses are more characteristic of the better class accommo-

[1] "A tenement house is any house or building, or portion thereof, which is rented, leased, let or hired out, to be occupied or is occupied as a home or residence of three families or more living independently of each other, and doing their cooking upon the premises, or by more than two families upon any floor, so living and cooking, but having a common right to the halls, stairways, yards, water-closets or privies, or some of them." Laws of New York, 1901, ch. 334. Legally this term covers multiple unit dwellings of all classes, cost and location.

[2] "Railroad" apartments are so called because they run the depth of the building without an interior hall and it is necessary to go through one room to get to the next, as in a train of cars.

dations than are apartment buildings, and much of the new housing in these boroughs is of this type. Thus, in comparing the necessary outlay for housing, by families at any standard of living, the type most prevalent in the separate boroughs for that standard must be priced so far as possible and relative rents must be computed on that basis.

Sources of Rent Data

Information on which the final estimates regarding rents were based was secured and checked in a number of ways. Real estate operators were consulted for their figures on rents for housing of the kind specified. In all, 123 brokers furnished estimates regarding representative rents in New York City, distributed as follows: Bronx, 21; Brooklyn, 27; Manhattan, 25; Queens, 39; Richmond, 11. Advertisements of apartments to rent, in two of the newspapers having extensive listings, were followed for several weeks; advertisements in other papers were followed less systematically; estimates and records of social and industrial organizations were obtained. Finally, the housing offered for rent was inspected by agents of the Board as prospective tenants. The data thus assembled and checked afford adequate representation of the rent situation. It should be borne in mind, however, that the figures given do not show the rents actually being paid but are, rather, the rents which are being asked of new tenants in the houses offered. It should further be borne in mind that not every house available in every borough was considered; indeed, that only samples in certain sections of the city were covered. So far as can be ascertained, however, these samples are adequate and there is every reason to believe that the estimates finally made are as representative as any figures can be without a complete census.

Rents in the Bronx

A larger proportion of the houses in the Bronx are so-called tenements than in any other borough except Manhattan. Unlike Manhattan and Brooklyn, however, the Bronx tenements are for the most part new law houses, as the majority of them have been built in the last fifteen or twenty years, since the subways were opened, and many of them are very high class apartment buildings. More than twice as many people in the Bronx live in multiple family dwellings as in single unit houses and more than three times as many are in the large houses as are in two-family buildings. Such being the case, the character of the appearance of the Bronx is given by its rows and rows of brick buildings, four or five stories high, in solid blocks, and housing hundreds of people. In the older sections smaller frame dwellings are still found, and in some there are streets with large frame houses set in lawns, with trees and shrubbery. The latter are rapidly disappearing, however, before the modern invasion. The East Bronx, comprising only a few years ago country estates and farm lands, is now being built up with one and two family dwellings and tenements. Many of these are of brick, and the appearance of some streets is not unlike that in the western section of Queens, while others resemble the older sections of the Bronx in their solid phalanxes of brick tenements.

Real estate brokers and social organizations were consulted and houses were inspected in Tremont, Fordham and Bedford Park in the West Bronx and in Westchester, Unionport, Van Nest, and in sections north, east and west of 149th Street in the East Bronx. These areas cover a variety of housing types and are believed adequately to represent the rent situation in that borough. It is not claimed that housing could not be obtained for less than the average minimum quoted and it is certain that more would often be required. It is believed, however, that the figures given are representative. Four-room, "cold water flats"[1] in the Bronx, in frame or brick houses, with baths but no heat, in the spring of 1926 rented for $30 to $40 a month, depending on their location, both as to neighborhood and within the house. An average of $8.50 a room was apparently a fair minimum for satisfactory accommodations. In heated apartments of the older type three rooms were renting for about $32, four rooms for $40 and five rooms for $52. The average was about $10.50 a room. In new two family brick houses, six rooms and sun

[1] "Cold water flats" are apartments in which the tenant supplies his own heat and hot water; there is no central system.

porch rented for $75 to $100; this included heat. In the larger new houses rents ranged from $15 a room up; the average minimum was about $16. Houses of the same type in somewhat better neighborhoods but which had been lived in for a few years cost about $50 for three rooms and $60 for four rooms; new houses in the same neighborhoods rented for about $20 a room as an average minimum.

Rents in Brooklyn

Brooklyn, which has the largest population of any of the five boroughs, and is next to the largest in area, was an important city years before its consolidation with the other boroughs to form the present city of New York. In the older sections, miles of streets of brown stone English basement houses and brick, stone or frame apartment houses in two, three or six family units of the railroad type of construction parallel in many respects similar housing of the same period, 40 or 50 years ago, in Manhattan. While this housing has often been improved by the introduction of electric light, the installation of bath rooms and occasionally, central heat, it is dark and awkward in layout, in comparison with the new housing, and lacks many so-called modern improvements. These houses, nevertheless, are conveniently located as to transportation, are often on wide streets with fine old trees, frequently they have front or back yards with grass plots, trees or garden and many of the neighborhoods are considered socially desirable.

Newer sections of Brooklyn contain many beautiful frame houses set in large yards on parked streets flanked with trees and shrubbery. Here, also, are found the better class of two family houses and the older high class apartment buildings. In these sections, however, the modern apartment house is rapidly making inroads and areas that not so many years ago were quite suburban are now being rebuilt with high class multiple unit dwellings. Still other sections of Brooklyn, where the land has never before been developed, are being rapidly built up with inexpensive frame or brick houses for one, two or sometimes more families. These are of the detached, semi-detached or row type, and the owner frequently lives in one apartment, renting out the others.

In these new developments the streets are usually paved, and in those of several years standing yards are green and trees along the streets are thriving. On the whole, Brooklyn housing is fairly well divided between dwellings of the one and two family type, and large tenements.

In a borough so populous and covering so large an area as Brooklyn it would obviously have been out of the question in a survey of this kind to have covered the entire territory. Real estate operators were consulted and houses were inspected in the following sections: Bushwick, East New York, Canarsie, Sheepshead Bay, Bay Ridge, Flatbush, Park Slope, Gowanus. From the data thus assembled it appears that the older housing contains larger apartments than the newer; indeed, only in the newest houses were units of three rooms and bath generally found. The older apartments contain four, five, and six rooms. For a cold water flat with bath, in three or six family houses, the minimum rent required averaged about $7.50 per room in the spring of 1926. This would provide for electricity, but the tenant would have to furnish his own heat and hot water from coal, oil or gas stoves in his own apartment. For $11 a room ($55 for five rooms; $45 for four rooms) very similar accommodations might be secured, with heat and hot water supplied by the landlord from a central heating system. These apartments were in old houses, but they were in good repair, decent neighborhoods and often were on attractive streets, conveniently located in relation to the business centers of the borough. Better accommodations in houses of the modern type but several years old could be had for about $15 a room ($75 for five rooms, $60 for four rooms; $50 for three rooms); and in new, two family houses, the rent was about the same. Floors of five rooms and porch in two family houses were found, with heat furnished by the landlord, at $12.50 a room; where the tenant had his own furnace it might not be quite so much. High class modern apartments in new buildings and good neighborhoods rented for $20 a room as an average minimum ($60 for three rooms; $80 for four rooms); a few were found for less after diligent search. Of the rents quoted above, the first two and the last refer to accommodations of which there seemed to be an adequate supply; for the apartments renting for $12.50 to $15 a room "shopping" was necessary. While they were to be found by careful hunting, none of the brokers consulted had many such places on their lists. It is possible that accommodations of the different types specified might have been found for less money; it is certain that much more could have been spent if desired. The figures given are thought to be fair averages for the type of housing specified.

Rents in Manhattan

Manhattan is essentially a borough of multi-family dwellings. From the oldest tenements downtown to the newest homes of fashion, Manhattan lives in layers. These may be single family houses converted to provide shelter for more than the original plan called for, they may be larger units, accommodating four, six, eight or more families to a floor and rising to a usual maximum of five stories in the air if they are walk-ups and much higher if elevators are provided. In between, in all sections of the borough, are found single family dwellings, sometimes whole rows of brown stone fronts with English basements; sometimes rows or single houses of very old brick construction. The characteristic Manhattan house, however, is the large tenement.

Minimum housing in Manhattan is, therefore, found in the tenements. But the actually existing minimum still used for habitation does not meet the requirements of this survey. Not only are many of them very old, insanitary and out of repair, but a surprisingly large number of them are without baths. A study made early in 1926 of 882 families under the care of one of the social organizations in the borough showed over three-quarters were living in apartments without a bath or central heat. These, of course, were relief cases in most instances, but visits made in the present investigation to a large number of houses in Manhattan occupied by working class families of some means indicated that private baths, for the exclusive use of a single family, are exceedingly rare in the older houses.

The sections in which real estate brokers were consulted and houses were inspected in Manhattan were Yorkville, the West Side south of 59th Street, Manhattanville and lower

Washington Heights. In the two mid-town neighborhoods, the apartments are of the old railroad type, three or more stories high, four apartments to a floor, with dark rooms and toilets in the halls, one for the use of two apartments, or in the basement. Many of the apartments do not contain bath-rooms, although the combination of bath-tub and wash-tub in the kitchen was sometimes offered as a substitute. White sinks and electricity are the "improvements" offered in these neighborhoods; sometimes, hot water. To get an apartment with a bath of its own, at least $8.50 a room was required ($42 for five rooms; $35 for four rooms) in the spring of 1926. Such an apartment would probably have electricity, and might have windows opening on an interior court; there might or might not be hot water. In Yorkville, few of these old places have central heat, and there are not enough on the West Side to consider the prices charged in these two districts as representative of rents of the older houses with "all improvements." Both of these neighborhoods are undergoing great changes, the East Side experiencing a boom in high-class residential building, the West Side being affected by the westward march of the theatrical district. For housing representative of the sort occupied by the families of office workers in Manhattan, the walk-up apartment houses erected twenty or more years ago in Manhattanville and the southern part of Washington Heights were inspected. These places, with heat, hot water and electricity but not many modern contrivances, which add to the cost in the places now being built, rented for about $12 a room ($60 for five rooms; $50 for four rooms). In more modern houses a few year old $15 a room was required ($60 for four rooms; $50 for three rooms) and such places must be searched for. The cheapest new place rented for $20 a room ($80 for four rooms; $60 for three rooms) and these prices were not found in the houses making any pretense to style.

Rents in Queens

Queens as a borough is a combination of a number of very old residence and business centers which date back to pre-revolutionary days, of more recent suburban settlements, and of very new developments in subdivisions which less than half a dozen years ago were truck farms or marshes. Thus the appearance of Queens differs greatly from section to section. Some of it is very attractive, with streets shaded by old trees, substantial, even pretentious houses setting back in fine gardens, or the newer high class residential developments, often of an apartment house type, which give an air of dignity and substance of a different kind. Some of Queens is old and not so attractive, with cheaper houses and run down neighborhoods or undeveloped lots held for price advancement.

Most characteristic of Queens, at least to the casual observer, is the mile after mile of newly built one and two family houses. In the western section of the borough these are of brick, and while very similar in architecture, there is enough difference to avoid monotony. Further out, they are of frame construction, exactly alike except possibly for color or shape of roof, setting four or five to a hundred feet of land and stretching for block after block with unrelieved uniformity. Some of these have garages; some streets are not paved even if they are graded, and, except in the older localities, there is no sewerage system and cesspools are the rule.

Larger units are also being built in Queens. These are of every grade, from old style brick railroad apartments with all improvements except heat, to very high class apartment houses. An interesting feature of the Queens building boom is the development of a number of model communities, built to indicate what can be done through careful planning in the way of providing comfort and beauty at minimum cost.

Many of the newly built houses are single family dwellings, occupied by the owner; some of them are two family units in which the owner lives on one floor and rents the other, sometimes furnishing heat, sometimes providing the tenant with a furnace of his own. This new housing in Queens appeals to a variety of purses and social standards. Houses or apartments in some of the developments are for sale and in some they are for rent; among those that were covered in this survey there were few vacancies and in one group, providing something more than 2,000 apartments, the waiting list was said to grow by 30 or 40 applicants each day.

Real estate brokers, social and business organizations were consulted and houses were inspected in Astoria, Long Island City, Flushing, Jamaica and Hollis. Here, as elsewhere, minimum housing was found in the older frame structures; there were practically no vacancies in these places and few houses could, therefore, be inspected because none were for rent. To find vacancies would require careful hunting. Such as were to be had would rent for $7 to $10 a room, with the tenant furnishing his own heat. Taking the average for the borough, the minimum cost of housing in Queens in the spring of 1926 may be placed at $40 per month for five rooms, unheated. In the newer houses, five rooms cost from $50 as a minimum in the flimsy frame structures, with the tenant furnishing his own heat, to $75 for six rooms in the brick buildings, with heat included. A minimum of $12.50 per room for such a place was a fair average; this included heat. For smaller units,those of three or four rooms, $15 a room ($60 for four rooms; $50 for three rooms) was the average minimum. For $12 a room, a few apartments were to be had in the older houses. In the buildings which have been converted from one or two family units into three family houses, the rent may also include electricity and the location may be more attractive than the houses in the new developments. Apartments in the large new modern houses rented for $20 a room up, but there were enough renting for $60 for three rooms and $80 for four rooms to set this figure as a minimum.

Rents in Richmond

Richmond, commonly known as Staten Island, is the most rural of any of the five boroughs of the city of New York, although from the point of view of initial settlement it is one of the oldest. Farms of considerable acreage in the center of the island are still raising produce which is shipped into Manhattan each day and in many more populous centers cows and chickens are fairly common. Its extensive shore front makes Staten Island a popular summer playground but there is also a permanent population of over 100,000.

Lacking transportation to the other boroughs or to the almost contiguous New Jersey except by ferry, Staten Island has not experienced the building booms attendant on the development of rapid transit in other sections of the city. Its industries are located at the North and West where communication with New Jersey is quite close, and such of the city's industrial population as live on Staten Island for the most part work there or in the immediately adjacent Perth Amboy, Elizabethport and Bayonne; commuters from the island are generally employed in the offices of Manhattan and Brooklyn.

Most of Staten Island lives in single family frame dwellings. These houses are of all ages, from little old places antedating the revolution to more flimsy places of recent construction. Many of them are owned by their occupants. While not experiencing a boom in any sense such as is found in some of the other boroughs, a large number of dwellings have been constructed in the last year or two, of both the single family and two family type. Values are far higher than they were a few years ago, in anticipation of bridges to New Jersey and a subway under the Narrows.

Real estate brokers were consulted in New Brighton and Port Richmond. They handle property all over the island. Settlements are so scattered that in inspecting houses for rent attention was concentrated on Port Richmond and Stapleton. It is possible that further from the ferries rents may be lower than those quoted in the more convenient locations, but the figures are apparently representative.

The typical frame house of a fair minimum grade on Staten Island is said to have five rooms, a furnace, bath, water and gas and in the spring of 1926 rented for $7 a room ($35 a month for five rooms). Floors in houses where the tenant furnishes his own heat from a separate furnace in the cellar, or unheated apartments over stores and in multiple unit buildings, rented in the average at the same rate. Houses and apartments in somewhat better buildings or locations cost a dollar or two more per room. There are relatively few heated apartments to rent in Richmond borough except in the new high-class houses. These were as expensive as in

TABLE 2: REPRESENTATIVE MINIMUM RANGE AND REPRESENTATIVE AVERAGE MINIMUM RENT PER ROOM PER MONTH FOR SPECIFIED TYPES OF HOUSING IN NEW YORK CITY, 1926[a]

(National Industrial Conference Board)

Type of Housing	Bronx		Brooklyn		Manhattan		Queens		Richmond	
	Range	Average	Range	Average	Range	Average	Range	Average	Range	Average
Single frame house	[b]	[b]	[b]	[b]	[b]	[b]	$8–10	$10.00	$6 up	$7.00
Two family house										
With heat	$10–15	$12.50	$10–15	$12.50	[b]	[b]	10–15	12.50	8–12	9.00
Without heat	8–10	8.50	[b]	[b]	[b]	[b]	10–12	10.00	6–11	7.00
Multiple family house										
Cold water, no bath	[b]		4–6	5.00	$4–7	$5.00	5–6	5.00	4–7	5.00
Cold water, bath	7.50–10	8.50	6–9	7.50	7–10	8.50	7–10	8.00	6–10	7.00
Heated, old	10–12	10.50	9–12	11.00	11–18	12.00	10–15	12.00	[b]	[b]
Heated, modern, old	10–15	15.00	15–18	15.00	15 up	15.00	[b]	[b]	[b]	[b]
Heated, modern, new	15–25	16.00	18 up	20.00	20 up	20.00	15–25	15.00	15 up	20.00

[a] These are the rents quoted for the type of house specified; a number of variables make any comparison of identical accommodations impossible.

[b] Not included.

the other boroughs, although it is possible that for a given outlay the tenant might secure better value.

Summary

The necessary minimum outlay for various types of housing in the separate boroughs of New York City is summarized in Table 2. As indicated there, this differs from place to place and although efforts were made to estimate the cost of securing identical accommodations in different localities, this was soon abandoned as impracticable. Not only were single frame houses not found in one place or old heated apartments in another, but the size and age of the buildings, character of the neighborhoods, conveniences provided and other considerations all affected the rents, even for the same general type of accommodation. The relatively inexpensive modern apartments in small units such as were found in quantities in certain sections of Queens were not found in any of the other boroughs except Brooklyn and this type was not usual there. The types that are omitted from the table entirely for some places were not listed either because they were not worth considering in that specific locality or because they were not visited in the final check up.

A few points are worth emphasizing in this summary of the rent situation. The first and most important is that these are the estimated average minimum rents which would be charged new tenants moving into the accommodations listed. Tenants who have been in the same house or apartment for a number of years would probably not be paying so much as the figures given in the table. The necessity for moving, however, be it either to another place in the same community or to the same type of house in another community would almost certainly require the payment of a rent higher than that previously paid. A counterbalancing tendency in rents for certain types of housing is the growing practice of granting concessions of rent for a month or more as an inducement to occupancy. This is not to be counted on for popular types of accommodations, however, but rather for those of which there is a considerable surplus; and the family which moves at the present time, no matter where it comes from or where it goes, is likely to pay more than it previously did for accommodations comparable to those it had been occupying for a number of years.

Another point to remember is that, in general, units of only three or four rooms are usually found in the multiple unit houses, whereas more rooms of this same grade usually are to be found as floors in two family dwellings and in the older heated apartments. Moreover, the fewer the number of rooms, the higher the rate per room. For this reason, apparently, families often rent the larger places and take in lodgers in order to get their own rent for a minimum. The figures quoted in the table are the rates for the prevailing number of rooms in the specified type of housing in the spring of 1926. The necessary outlay for rents by families of different size, age and occupation is summarized in Chapters VI and VIII.

CHAPTER II

FUEL AND LIGHT

Coal, Gas, Kerosene

THE custom of supplying heat in return for a part of the rent is so prevalent in New York City apartments that only in the oldest and cheapest houses does the tenant in a multiple unit dwelling heat his own premises. The latter, so-called cold water flats, are warmed in several ways. In many apartments it has been customary to have a coal stove of some sort in the living room, which, with heat from the kitchen range, kept the place fairly comfortable. In the winter of 1925–1926 coal was so high, however, that kerosene frequently was used in its place for heating. Gas, also, is often used to heat rooms not warmed from a coal range or furnace and some of the gas companies reported a greatly increased consumption in 1925–1926, coincident with the rise in the price of coal.

The price of coal differs very slightly if at all between the separate boroughs and greatly according to the way in which it is bought. In May, 1926, the usual price of stove coal in all five boroughs was $14.75 a ton when delivered from a wagon; nut or egg was sometimes the same, sometimes $14.50. When the tenant has a furnace of his own, as in certain single or two family houses in Queens or Richmond, he customarily buys his coal in ton lots or fractions thereof and stores it in the cellar. Where, however, many families live in the same house and heat is furnished from a stove in the apartment, it is not always convenient to store coal in large quantities or to haul it up from a subterranean bin whenever it is required. Hence, in these houses coal frequently is purchased in small lots which can be carried to the apartment by the dealer and kept there until used.[1] Many families of small income also

[1] It is claimed that while there is storage place for a ton of coal for each apartment in these large cold water flat buildings it is seldom used; others hold that the price of coal in the winter of 1925–1926 taught the more thrifty to buy in larger quantities.

buy their coal in this way because they cannot lay out the price of even a quarter ton at one time. Coal bought in small lots is very expensive as contrasted with ton lot purchases. In the Bronx, Brooklyn and Manhattan, for example, where coal for the cold water flats is customarily purchased in 50 lb. or 100 lb. bags, its cost when bought from a peddler was from $1 to $1.20 a hundred in May, 1926, which is at an average rate of $22 a ton, as contrasted with $14.50 or $14.75 a ton when bought in ton lots and delivered from a wagon.

Kerosene cost 20 cents a gallon in many places, 21 cents in others. Its consumption as a substitute for coal seemed to be confined largely to Manhattan and certain sections of Brooklyn.

The rates for gas differed, not only among the separate boroughs but among the different companies within a borough, depending ordinarily on the average density of the population served. As a rule the number of customers served at the higher rate is far less than the number served at the lower rate. The following are the rates per thousand for gas for domestic use charged in the separate boroughs in the spring of 1926:

Bronx	$1.15, $1.45
Brooklyn	$1.15, $1.30
Manhattan	$1.15
Queens	$1.15, $1.30, $1.38
Richmond	$1.45

It was reported by the companies with the highest rates that the extensive use of gas for heating at the present time was not feasible in the territories they served because the cost would be almost prohibitive.

Such reports as could be gathered regarding the relative consumption of coal, gas and kerosene, when used for heat in cold water flats were not sufficiently accurate to weight the prices of the different fuel items. One woman in Brooklyn reported that she spent 50 cents a day for gas during the winter; another in Manhattan used a gallon of kerosene a day, another in Brooklyn bought a 50 lb. bag of coal every other day. Dealers reported the consumption of coal in the cold water flats to vary all the way from 100 lbs. to 400 lbs. a week during the winter. Others reported that five or six room apartments in the neighborhood used from two to two and one-half tons of coal a season. Floors in frame houses were reported to require from somewhat more to somewhat less than a ton a room to heat. Reports on the use of kerosene were more uniform, one gallon a day being generally reported as the average consumption per family where one coal stove and one kerosene stove were used.

The report on the cost of living in Manhattan, prepared in 1915 by the Bureau of Personal Service of the New York City Board of Estimate and Apportionment[1] estimated that during the winter months averaging 18 weeks, three 50 lb. bags of coal a week and 6 bundles of wood were necessary for a four room apartment, and that during 13 weeks in the fall two 50 lb. bags of coal and four bundles of wood would be sufficient. This is equivalent to two tons a year and was all the heat allowed. Family welfare organizations in New York in 1926 were allowing 200 lbs. of coal a week in the winter and 100 lbs. in the spring and fall, which totals slightly more than two tons a year. Some kerosene or gas is also used although, as already indicated, the relative consumption is uncertain.

The best estimate that can be made of fuel consumption in the four room cold water flats in rows in the Bronx, Brooklyn and Manhattan, and its cost at prices prevailing in the spring of 1926, seems to be as follows:

Two tons coal at $22	$44.00
Charcoal or wood for kindling	5.00
Kerosene (18 weeks at $1.40)	25.20
	$74.20

If gas were used with coal instead of kerosene, the cost would be somewhat less, an average of 3,000 or 4,000 cubic feet a month being sufficient for one gas heater. In Queens and Richmond, where the housing is more exposed, somewhat more fuel for heating is required, but coal here is usually bought in ton or half ton lots, at a considerably lower rate.[2]

[1] New York City, Board of Estimate and Apportionment, Report on the Cost of Living for an Unskilled Laborer's Family in New York City, submitted by the Bureau of Standards to the Committee on Salary and Grades, 1915.

[2] Coal is sometimes sold at the yard in small amounts to customers who will cart it away themselves but the rate is the same as for ton lots delivered.

An allowance of $59 for four tons of coal at $14.75 per ton and $5 for kindling would, therefore, probably adequately represent the necessary allowance for this item in the houses in these boroughs, where the tenant customarily heats his own premises, either by stoves or by a furnace in the cellar.[1]

For three rooms, one bedroom being eliminated, the same amount of fuel would probably be consumed in a cold water flat as was burned to heat four rooms, since the same stoves would be used. It is fair to presume, however, that a family having one bedroom more than is needed would get some income from the room and that the occupant thereof would have the benefit of such heat as was furnished. Such being the case the allowance for fuel for four rooms in a cold water flat has been reduced 10% to get the estimated requirement for three. For the houses or apartments in Queens and Richmond, heated by furnace, the same reduction in fuel allowance has been made. If an extra bedroom is added, 10% may be added to the fuel allowance.

In cold water flats the coal range which heats the apartment is customarily used during more than half the year for cooking also. During the 21 weeks when this is not in use, the average minimum consumption of gas for cooking and heating water may be placed at about 2,000 cubic feet per month. Calling this five months, the annual cost, based on the lowest rates in each borough, would average $11.50 in the Bronx, Brooklyn, Manhattan and Queens. In Richmond, with its single high rate, the cost would be $14.50. In the steam heated apartments and many houses heated by a furnace, gas is used for cooking the year around. At the rate of 2,000 cubic feet per month, the cost would be $27.60 in the Bronx, Brooklyn, Manhattan and Queens and $34.80 in Richmond.

Electricity

Although some apartments were still found to be lighted by gas, for the most part electricity has been installed in even the oldest houses. The rates per kilowatt hour for domestic

[1] Nut coal used in the stoves in some cases costs less than stove coal used in the furnace; the price quoted is for stove coal.

use, as charged by the different companies, were as follows in the separate boroughs in the spring of 1926:

Bronx . . . . . . 7 cents, plus coal charge; 11 cents, with minimum of $1 per month; 12 cents
Brooklyn. . . . 7½ cents, plus coal charge, with minimum of $1 per month
Manhattan . . 7 cents, plus coal charge
Queens. . . . . . 9 cents, with minimum of $1 per month; 11 cents
Richmond . . . 10 cents, with minimum of $1 per month

The higher rates for the most part were in the less populous sections of the newer boroughs where economies of large scale service have not yet become possible.

The minimum consumption of electricity was estimated by the different companies at different quantities, depending to some extent on the rate. One of the largest companies, with a low rate, reported that of 180,000 customers the majority used 15 kwh. per month, although the consumption most frequently found was 10 kwh. Another large company, with a low rate, reported that on their books were over 50,000 accounts averaging less than 50 cents a month. A representative minimum was placed by this company at 17 kwh. per month; this, however, covered the use of appliances.

Since in four of the five boroughs there was a minimum charge for electricity of $1 per month, regardless of the amount used, an allowance of $1 a month was made for this item in the cold water flats in all boroughs. This would permit the consumption of more electricity where the rates were lowest, a fairly common experience, it would provide for the very small coal charges of the companies having this addition to the rate, and it would still permit even the residents of Richmond with the 10-cent rate to use 10 kwh. a month as a minimum.

For families living in houses with a central heating system, more rooms are probably used than in the so-called cold water flats where the family necessarily congregates about the one or two sources of warmth. For these centrally heated houses, a small additional allowance has been made for electricity, based on the average minimum use of 15 kwh. per month in a house or an apartment of four rooms. Taking 15 kwh. as the minimum consumption of electricity per month in such a house or apartment, multiplying that by 12 and then by the lowest rates noted above, gives the following as the average minimum cost of electricity per year in the separate boroughs of New York City for four rooms in centrally heated housing:

Bronx	$13.10[a]
Brooklyn	14.00[b]
Manhattan	13.10[c]
Queens	16.20
Richmond	18.00

[a] At lowest rate is $12.60; 50 cents added for coal. Customers served at higher rate presumably use less electricity.
[b] Rate is $13.50; 50 cents added for coal.
[c] Rate is $12.60; 50 cents added for coal.

The elimination or addition of one bedroom would change the electricity bill but little, since such rooms as would be affected are not heated enough to serve as sitting rooms. Moreover, in as much as a number of the companies require a minimum payment, regardless of the quantity of electricity used, the outlay for three rooms would be the same as for four, except in Manhattan and certain sections of the Bronx. The addition of one room would add only a dollar or two per year to the electricity bills.

The estimated cost of heating and lighting three or four rooms in the separate boroughs of New York City, at prices and rates current in the spring of 1926, is summarized in Table 3.

Summary

The basic data regarding the cost of heating and lighting the houses and apartments described in Chapter I are so diverse and the combinations possible so numerous, that certain assumptions were necessarily made in order to permit any estimate of minimum outlay. These assumptions were that the cold water flats in the large houses in the Bronx, Brooklyn and Manhattan were heated by the kitchen range, supplemented either by gas or kerosene and that the more exposed frame houses in Queens and Richmond were heated solely by coal, sometimes from stoves, sometimes from a furnace; that in many of them coal was used for cooking as well as for heating during part of the year, but that for a

TABLE 3: AVERAGE MINIMUM COST OF COAL, KEROSENE, GAS AND ELECTRICITY PER YEAR FOR HOUSES AND APARTMENTS OF DIFFERENT SIZES AND DIFFERENT TYPES IN NEW YORK CITY, 1926

(National Industrial Conference Board)

Service required for—	Bronx	Brooklyn	Manhattan	Queens	Richmond
Unheated house or apartment					
Coal, gas, kerosene, kindling					
Three rooms	$66.78[a]	$66.78[a]	$66.78[a]	$57.60[a]	$57.60[a]
Four rooms	74.20	74.20	74.20	64.00	64.00
Gas for cooking	11.50	11.50	11.50	11.50	14.50
Electricity[b]					
Three rooms	10.80[a]	12.00	10.80[a]	12.00	12.00
Four rooms	12.00	12.00	12.00	12.00	12.00
Heated apartment					
Gas for cooking	27.60	27.60	27.60	27.60	34.80
Electricity[b]					
Three rooms	11.79[a]	12.60[a]	11.79[a]	14.58[a]	16.20[a]
Four rooms	13.10	14.00	13.10	16.20	18.00

[a] A reduction of 10% from the necessary outlay for four rooms.

[b] Although the rates charged by different companies in the separate boroughs varied, the estimated cost to minimum domestic consumers was not so different as the difference in rates would suggest, due to allowance for the fact that some of them had the same minimum monthly charge, regardless of the rate and also that the consumption of electricity seems to vary with the rate, and hence bills are about the same, at a given standard, more or less regardless of the rate.

period of five months gas was used for cooking and heating hot water; that electricity was used for lighting.

The minimum cost of gas and electricity used in steam heated apartments occupied by office workers in the Bronx, Brooklyn and Manhattan was also estimated. In Queens and Richmond, steam heated places are not the most characteristic housing for minimum standard office workers. The cost of heating and lighting the one and two family frame houses in which these families usually live was, therefore, estimated on a somewhat different basis from that used for the older steam heated apartments in the Bronx, Brooklyn and Manhattan. The combinations adopted and final estimates are given in Chapters VI and VIII.

CHAPTER III

FOOD

Minimum Food Requirements

THE average family in New York City, as apparently in other sections of the country, lives on an extremely restricted and relatively expensive diet. This is not because they have so little or so much to spend for food but because the elements of nutrition are not yet common knowledge and tastes have been cultivated for only certain types of food. With the increasing pressure of high rents, the effect of this limitation of diet is particularly noticeable. Families have been obliged to cut down their expenditures for food but they are still following an expensive diet while going without the essentials of a balanced ration. Storekeepers throughout the city noted the difficulty they had in selling the cheaper cuts of meat, while others referred to diets of bread and herring or bread and soup, as being the result of high rents.

The requirements for adequate nourishment and variety in food consumption have been standardized as have no other essentials in the cost of living. The number of calories required to provide properly for the needs of persons of different sex, age and occupation, and their necessary distribution among meats, fish, eggs, milk, cereals, fruits and vegetables, sweets and fatty foods so as to get the proper proportion of protein, calcium, phosphorus and iron has been determined through exhaustive experiments and experience. While there is some variation in the final allowances made by different students for differences in sex, age and occupation, the net results for a family composed of persons of varied ages and both sexes are not far apart.

In the present study of the cost of living, an effort has been made to prepare a well-balanced food budget, based largely on the less expensive foods. Such a diet will provide all the nourishment and variety necessary, at a minimum cost. Some relatively expensive items are included, but the body of the food allowance is made up of the less costly foods. It should be understood, of course, that the items listed are to a considerable extent types representative of year round consumption. When fruits and vegetables other than those given are at their lowest prices, some of them may be used instead of those noted here. Other varieties of meat or fish at approximately the prices quoted will yield approximately the same nourishment. But for the amounts allowed, based on this list, an entirely satisfactory dietary may be arranged.

Price Data

The questionnaire used in collecting food prices lists 40 separate items. So far as possible these are supposed to be for bulk not package goods, of the grades usually purchased by wage earners. These items were priced personally by agents of the Board in both the East and West Bronx; Bushwick and Park Slope in Brooklyn; Yorkville and the West Side of Manhattan below 59th Street; Astoria, Long Island City, Flushing and Jamaica in Queens and Stapleton in Richmond. In addition, every important chain of food stores in the city furnished quotations. Thus, the prices used represent quotations from cash and carry, as well as credit and delivery stores and a few street venders. Together they cover more than 3,000 stores in the five boroughs of New York City.

When the prices had been secured for the 40 items listed, the arithmetic average of each was found for the neighborhood stores and for the chain stores in each borough. These were then averaged, thus giving chain stores and neighborhood stores equal weight in the final price. These average prices for the separate items were then multiplied by the quantity of each allowed in the budget to find the cost of a balanced food allowance. As the method used in reaching these conclusions regarding the minimum cost of food for families of various sizes differs from that usually employed in estimating the cost of living among wage earners, it is necessary to present a somewhat detailed explanation.

Quantity Data

As already noted, the measuring units hitherto taken to estimate the cost of living of wage earners have been a family of two adults and three children under 14 years of age; a single woman taking all of her meals apart from a family group; and a single man in the same circumstances. It was noted that this is not the representative New York City living arrangement, since the average New York City family apparently contains two wage earners and only a little more than one child 14 years of age or under. For purposes of measuring the cost of living, therefore, it may be assumed that, regardless of how this cost is met, it is established on the requirements of two parents, a grown daughter or a grown son, and one or two children 14 years of age or under.

From the point of view of food consumption, worked out on a calorie basis, the requirements of one child between the ages of 11 and 14 are about equal to those of two children aged between 7 and 10, and 3 or under[1]; and these in turn are equivalent to approximately eight-tenths the needs of a grown man at moderately active labor. The food requirements of a woman are variously placed at eight- or nine-tenths those of a man. The quantity and kinds of food consumed also depend largely on the kind of work done, and the needs of a man or woman at relatively heavy labor are considerably greater than are those of persons at more sedentary occupations. The energy needed, therefore, by an industrial worker at moderately heavy labor, and by his wife doing all of the work of caring for his family, will be proportionally more than those for a man at lighter office work and his family where some assistance with the housework is provided. A girl at light factory labor and one at office work have much the same food requirements. Disregarding for the moment the question as to who is to pay for the food consumed, the requirements and their cost for one week may be analyzed.

Taking the needs of the industrial worker type of family, it may fairly be assumed that he at his work and his wife at hers are engaged in moderately active muscular labor. Under such conditions, the man requires 3,500 calories as purchased

[1] It is not necessary for the present purpose that the food consumption be worked out for children of every age.

per day,[1] the woman nine-tenths as much or 3,150 calories. Children, if in health, may be universally assumed to be actively employed. Thus, a boy of 12 or two children, 8 and 2, respectively, would need approximately 2,800 calories purchased per day. The calorie requirements of the grown son in the family, who may be presumed to be engaged at light work, and the grown daughter at light or sedentary work, may be placed at 3,150 and 2,835, respectively, purchased per day. The total for this family is 15,435 calories per day or 108,045 per week. In this, there must be protein food; fats and carbohydrates; meat and fish, fruit and vegetables, dairy products and cereals, milk and sugar.

Table 4 gives a balanced combination of these different types of inexpensive food stuffs, sufficient to provide nourishment and variety for four adults and one or two children for one week, and their cost at prices prevailing in the spring of 1926.[2] The items listed may not conform to the purchasing habits of many families of small income because, as already noted, the latter not only do not use the cheaper cuts of meat included, but they probably do not use so much milk or fresh fruits as is allowed here. If, however, individual taste requires more meat and less milk, more vegetables and less fruit, more bread and less cereal, the sums allowed may be redistributed to obtain similar results at relatively the same cost. They will not permit, however, the exclusive purchase of expensive meats, fruit and vegetables out of season, or elaborate bakery or delicatessen products.

Ice is sold from wagons in the more suburban areas of the city, but in the more populous sections it is quite frequently delivered in carts by the same peddlers who in the winter sell coal. While the large dealers report the rate per hundred pounds, the peddlers are more familiar with pieces at a given price. There is little difference in the cost of ice, whether

[1] Food purchased suffers considerable waste and shrinkage before it is transformed to heat units for the human body. While the loss varies as between the different kinds of food, the average is about 10%. To secure 3,000 calories of energy per man per day, therefore, approximately 3,500 calories worth of food would need to be purchased.

[2] The energy requirements on which the food allowances are predicated are based on data in the following: Mary Swartz Rose, "Feeding the Family," New York, 1917; *ibid.*, "Laboratory Manual of Dietetics," New York, 1913; Henry C. Sherman, "Chemistry of Food and Nutrition," New York, 1924.

TABLE 4: MINIMUM REQUIREMENTS AND AVERAGE MINIMUM COST OF FOOD FOR ONE WEEK, BASED ON THE NEEDS OF TWO MEN, TWO WOMEN, AND ONE OLDER CHILD UNDER 14 YEARS OF AGE, OR TWO YOUNGER CHILDREN, LIVING AT A FAIR AMERICAN STANDARD IN NEW YORK CITY, 1926

(National Industrial Conference Board)

Item	Quantity (in Pounds)	Cost in 1926				
		Bronx	Brooklyn	Manhattan	Queens	Richmond
Meat and fish						
Leg lamb	5	$1.69	$1.77	$1.69	$1.81	$1.86
Hamburger steak	1½	.35	.36	.31	.35	.40
Flank beef	1	.22	.24	.21	.24	.22
Pork chops	1½	.48	.48	.48	.51	.53
Bacon	½	.24	.24	.23	.24	.26
Bologna sausage	1	.31	.30	.29	.30	.30
Fresh fish	1½	.32	.32	.32	.33	.31
Dried cod	1	.33	.33	.32	.30	.30
Can salmon	1	.18	.18	.18	.17	.17
Dairy products						
Milk	14 qts.	2.10	2.10	2.13	2.11	2.07
Butter	2	1.03	1.00	1.02	.99	.97
Oleomargarine	1	.32	.30	.32	.31	.31
Lard	½	.11	.11	.11	.11	.11
Cheese	1	.40	.38	.39	.38	.37
Eggs	2 doz.	.77	.77	.77	.78	.78
Vegetables						
Potatoes	2 pks.	1.83	1.98	1.86	1.95	2.13
Carrots	3	.23	.22	.24	.23	.25
Onions	4	.22	.25	.23	.24	.26
Cabbage	4	.29	.28	.31	.31	.31
Dried beans	2	.23	.23	.24	.22	.22
Can tomatoes	2 1/16	.17	.17	.17	.17	.17
Cocoa	½	.18	.19	.18	.16	.18
Fruit						
Oranges	3 doz.	1.38	1.35	1.38	1.30	1.48
Bananas	¾ doz.	.22	.21	.22	.22	.23
Apples	6	.40	.42	.43	.39	.45
Raisins	1	.15	.15	.15	.14	.15
Prunes	2	.27	.29	.27	.28	.29
Dried apricots	1	.35	.33	.34	.33	.36
Bread, cereals, sugar						
White bread	15	1.31	1.29	1.31	1.29	1.28
Wheat flour	3	.22	.23	.22	.22	.23
Corn meal	1	.07	.07	.07	.07	.08
Rice	1	.11	.11	.11	.11	.12
Macaroni	1	.15	.15	.15	.16	.18
Rolled oats	3	.24	.24	.24	.23	.25
Soda crackers	1	.20	.19	.20	.19	.19
Granulated sugar	5	.29	.30	.29	.28	.30
Syrup	1	.10	.11	.12	.12	.12
Tea, coffee, etc.						
Tea	¼	.22	.19	.21	.18	.21
Coffee	1	.44	.44	.44	.44	.45
Condiments		.10	.10	.10	.10	.10
Ice		.20	.20	.20	.20	.20
Total		$18.42	$18.57	$18.45	$18.46	$19.15

TABLE 4: MINIMUM REQUIREMENTS AND AVERAGE MINIMUM COST OF FOOD FOR ONE WEEK, BASED ON THE NEEDS OF TWO MEN, TWO WOMEN, AND ONE OLDER CHILD UNDER 14 YEARS OF AGE, OR TWO YOUNGER CHILDREN, LIVING AT A FAIR AMERICAN STANDARD IN NEW YORK CITY, 1926 —(*Continued*)

Item	Quantity (in Pounds)	Cost in 1926				
		Bronx	Brooklyn	Manhattan	Queens	Richmond
Specific Requirements						
Man at moderately heavy work.......	22.65%	$4.17	$4.21	$4.18	$4.18	$4.34
Woman at moderately heavy work.......	20.39%	3.76	3.79	3.76	3.76	3.90
Man at light work...	20.39%	3.76	3.79	3.76	3.76	3.90
Woman at light work	18.35%	3.38	3.41	3.39	3.39	3.51
Boy, 12 years of age, or two children, age, respectively, 8 years and 2 years.......	18.22%	3.36	3.38	3.36	3.36	3.49
Total.......	100.00%	$18.43	$18.58	$18.45	$18.45	$19.14

bought from the large dealers or the peddlers, and on the whole, not sufficient variation as between the boroughs to warrant a difference in allowance, since dealers in separate sections of the same borough reported a range of prices comparable with the range reported from one borough to another. Sixty and 65 cents a hundred seemed to be the prevailing rates for ice in the springof 1926, although some quotations of 70 cents were obtained in Queens. The average family of small means apparently requires from 40 to 60 cents a week for ice during the season when it is taken. This expenditure is made as needed by the weather requirements, but probably is spread over about five months in all, less ice being taken in May and September and more in June, July and August. An allowance of 60 cents a week for ice, for approximately 18 weeks, is equivalent to 20 cents a week throughout the year, and would undoubtedly answer minimum requirements in all of the boroughs at prices prevailing in the spring of 1926.

Food condiments include all of the flavors and seasonings which make food palatable but have little or no nutriment. Salt, pepper, mustard, vinegar, vanilla, chili sauce, catsup, are examples of the items the outlay for condiments is supposed to cover. Ten cents a week allowed as a round sum will provide amply for these items.

Summary

The quantity and varieties of food required for males and females of different ages and in different kinds of occupations have been so well established that in attempting to estimate its minimum cost all that was necessary was to ascertain the articles which furnished most nourishment, palatability and variety for the least money and, having priced these in markets patronized by families of small and moderate means, combine these average prices with the quantities of each required. The data thus collected furnish the basis for estimating the minimum cost of food for families with a varying number of members, of different sex, age and occupation. These estimates are made in Chapters VI and VIII.

CHAPTER IV

CLOTHING

The Standard of Dress

THE standard of dress in New York City is high. It is not customary for men or women, boys or girls, to wear in public the sort of informal dress which is usual in many smaller industrial communities, especially those of the exclusively mill type. Men employed at manual labor may appear on the streets in clothing of a somewhat different kind from that worn by office workers, but their appearance is probably above the average for those in similar employment elsewhere. Among women factory employees it is usual to change from street to work clothes during business hours, and on the street there is little to distinguish their occupation by their appearance. Women at home have more opportunity for informal dress but this, also, is customarily trim, and the children are notably well kept and attractively dressed.

These effects have been achieved in recent years with increasing difficulty, not so much because of the high cost of clothing as because of high rents. Clothing dealers everywhere, but especially in the neighborhood stores, complained that the rents paid by their patrons were such as to necessitate a serious curtailment in customary purchases of clothing. This was confirmed by the experience of some of the social welfare agencies that clothing often was being worn beyond its usual period of use.

Thus the custom of buying cheap clothes and buying them often seems to be growing. The shops are full of garments which present an attractive appearance but of which the wearing qualities in some cases are problematical. Style changes, on the one hand, fostering a desire for rapid replacement, and lack of anything but the smallest sums available for outlay at any given time for any given garment, on the other, urge the purchase of the least expensive type of goods, even by persons considerably above the minimum standard of living.

Other changes in clothing customs have occurred in recent years also, notably in the case of women's clothing. These have taken several forms. Not only are there differences in the kinds of garments and the materials of which they are made, but there has been a considerable elimination. High shoes, except of an orthopedic variety, are hardly ever carried by New York shoe dealers; shirt waists and skirts are not worn as once they were except as suit combinations, and even the latter are far less popular than the dress and coat; underclothing is reduced to a minimum. On the other hand, it would be a poor family, indeed, which did not provide an occasional pair of silk stockings for its women folk; and fur, of a kind, on coats is well-nigh universal. Among men's and children's clothing fewer changes have been made, so that budgets established several years ago for them are not so greatly out of date.

Minimum Clothing Requirements

Clothing requirements have not been standardized as have those for food, nor can the quantity necessary under given conditions be so readily determined. Although studies have been made of the clothing actually used by different types of families in different localities, these are not up to date and, even in their day, they were not entirely authoritative as to whether the quantities used were sufficient because recognized standards of adequacy are lacking.[1] Thus, in making up clothing budgets for the purpose of measuring the cost of clothing one person's estimate is as good as another, provided the results are reasonable, and there are at hand a number of basic clothing budgets to which prevailing price quotations might be applied.[2]

[1] See, for example, United States Bureau of Labor Statistics, "Cost of Living in the United States," Bulletin No. 357, Washington, 1924, pp. 120–275.

[2] R. H. Macy and Company, "How Much Should I Spend for Clothes," New York, 1923; William Filene's Sons Company, "Clothing Budgets and How to Use Them," Boston, 1922; United States Bureau of Labor Statistics, "Tentative Quantity and Cost Budget," Washington, 1919; California State Civil Service Commission, Cost of Living Survey, Report, Sacramento, 1923; "A Method of Determining Adequate Clothing Allowances for Dependent and Low Income Families," issued jointly by the Charity Organization Society of New York, the New York Association for Improving the Condition of the Poor, and the United Hebrew Charities of New York, 1925.

None of these budgets seemed, for one reason or another, exactly to meet the needs of the present survey. All of them, however, were drawn on freely for suggestions for the make-up of a 1926 clothing budget for New York City, and while more of one item might be allowed here and less of another there, it seems probable that the net result would be about the same, if any reasonable budget were used for a specified standard of living.

From the point of view of constructing minimum clothing budgets, the problem is to determine what is really essential and what may be considered as catering merely to generally prevalent desires. Answers to this were based largely on experience, on common observation and on opinions of the shop keepers. From this evidence it appears that more and more clothing is being bought ready made and that, in many instances, leaving out of account quality, the ready made garments are as cheap as material can be purchased to make them at home. This is notably true of children's clothing and underwear. Other garments, on the other hand, such as women's dresses, may be made at home at less cost than they can be purchased ready made, and in most cases, apparently, the quality obtainable for a given outlay can be better secured through home dressmaking than through ready to wear purchases.

The clothing budgets used in this survey are complete revisions of the budgets used in the Board's earlier studies of the minimum cost of living, and have been designed to take account, so far as possible, of the conditions noted above. Although they differ in some respects from other clothing budgets hitherto published, they are thought to be fairly representative of minimum conditions in New York City in the spring of 1926. In any event, they are typical, not absolute, and in most cases the cost allowed may be adjusted to suit the ideas of those who think some other combinations of garments desirable. Two itemized budgets have been constructed for men, four for women and two each for children of three different ages, six children's clothing budgets in all. The quantity allowance and average replacement are based on the assumption that each garment will be worn out before being discarded and that social requirements are simple and

the demands for variety limited. Differences between the two married men's budgets and differences between those for the woman in the home and those for the woman at work are based largely on the requirements of occupation. Differences between the budgets for married and single men are taken care of by adding a flat percentage to the latter to cover differences in the cost of services when performed by a man's wife and when they must be paid for.

Price Data

The questionnaires used listed 31 items of men's clothing, 34 of women's, 62 of children's, and 12 yard goods items. In addition, data were collected on 4 shoe repairing items and 3 cleaning and pressing services.

The standard of quality specified on the clothing questionnaires used was "inexpensive but fair grades of merchandise such as is usually purchased by wage earners" and the prices secured were the lowest charged for these types of goods at the stores consulted.

In general, it is probable that shoes, hats, underwear and most accessories in all budgets are bought at neighborhood stores, and also a number of the articles in the men's and boy's clothing budgets. The larger items or those for which a greater selection is desired are frequently purchased in more general shopping centers. Accordingly, for this investigation, prices were secured from three types of stores: (1) stores in local shopping centers;[1] (2) stores in more general shopping centers; (3) chain stores located in either or both shopping districts.

The number of stores supplying quotations for clothing, counting the chain stores only once in each borough, was as follows:

Borough	*Number of Stores*
Bronx	72
Brooklyn	79
Manhattan	80
Queens	80
Richmond	26
Total	337

[1] The same local shopping centers were canvassed for clothing prices as those in which food prices were secured.

All of the stores included were those catering to the trade of persons of modest income, without regard to the prices charged, and the quotations secured often showed a considerable range, according to the character of the goods priced. Prices were collected from these stores by agents of the National Industrial Conference Board who called in person and priced the goods or secured the prices directly from the buyers. In no instance were sale or bargain quotations secured, but only minimum prices for the standards specified.

From the quotations thus secured, the arithmetic average price was calculated for each item. These average prices are given for each borough separately in Table 5. The clothing prices thus shown are based on regular stock, not special sales, bargains or markdowns. They are for new goods, not articles bought second hand or at rummage sales, although this is a fairly common practice in certain sections of the city. They are averages of all prices secured, not the lowest quotation for each item. Thus, in some ways, they are subject to discounts, because at times the items listed may be available below the regular market price, and in some stores, quotations lower than the average will be found. A counterbalancing tendency, however, may possibly be the purchase of clothing on the installment plan. While not studied extensively in the present investigation, enough was uncovered to indicate that the cost of garments purchased in this way is greater than when cash is paid.

Average prices for the articles listed, multiplied by the quantity of each allowed as the average annual replacement, are shown in Tables 10a to 10e, inclusive; Table 15; Tables 20a to 20e, inclusive, and Table 24. These balanced clothing budgets indicate the average cost of clothing for one year for individuals of different sex, age and occupation based on prices in the spring of 1926. In Tables 11 and 21 these are summarized so as to indicate the average annual cost of clothing for families with varying numbers, and for individuals at different occupations.

TABLE 5: AVERAGE MINIMUM RETAIL PRICES OF SELECTED ARTICLES OF WEARING APPAREL, YARD GOODS, CLOTHING ACCESSORIES AND SERVICES IN NEW YORK CITY, 1926

(National Industrial Conference Board)

Item	Bronx	Brooklyn	Manhattan	Queens	Richmond
Men's clothing					
Suit	$19.91	$19.62	$19.73	$20.40	$16.45
Overcoat	18.90	19.33	21.32	21.42	21.05
Extra trousers	3.42	3.88	3.86	3.14	3.37
Sweater	4.16	3.59	3.85	3.32	2.83
Madras shirt	1.41	1.47	1.54	1.47	1.45
Cotton work shirt	.97	.95	.95	.94	.94
Part wool work shirt	1.99	1.93	2.22	2.01	2.04
Overalls	2.73	3.02	2.89	2.92	2.42
Oxfords	4.76	4.73	4.84	4.58	3.77
High shoes	4.77	4.82	5.07	4.48	3.65
Work shoes	4.39	4.13	4.30	3.94	2.41
Rubbers	1.36	1.35	1.36	1.32	1.35
Part wool socks	.45	.41	.45	.42	.42
Cotton socks	.23	.22	.22	.19	.21
Summer union suit	1.17	.99	1.03	.98	.92
Winter union suit	1.48	1.41	1.48	1.49	1.48
Night clothes	1.43	1.42	1.37	1.33	1.38
Felt hat	3.42	3.03	2.96	3.41	3.29
Straw hat	2.19	1.80	1.96	1.74	1.80
Cap	1.39	1.23	1.06	1.26	1.10
Wool gloves	.94	.88	.86	.84	.87
Work gloves	.14	.15	.19	.20	.18
Kid gloves	2.07	2.26	1.96	2.10	2.14
Collar	.20	.19	.19	.20	.21
Tie	.70	.62	.73	.58	.52
Garters	.26	.25	.28	.25	.24
Belt	.57	.62	.65	.51	.47
Suspenders	.52	.49	.53	.47	.46
White handkerchief	.10	.09	.10	.09	.10
Colored handkerchief	.15	.14	.13	.12	.10
Umbrella	1.44	1.19	1.27	1.05	1.25
Women's clothing					
Coat	13.06	10.50	14.90	13.67	11.25
Suit	14.83	16.21	15.35	18.57	19.75
Sweater	3.15	2.30	3.30	3.68	2.32
Wool dress	10.01	5.83	6.29	8.12	7.50
Silk dress	9.98	7.14	8.32	8.84	9.61
Cotton dress	2.14	1.89	2.79	2.13	2.03
House dress	.86	.75	1.07	.97	1.15
Silk overblouse	4.40	3.30	4.04	4.09	3.87
Cotton overblouse	1.51	1.21	1.35	1.53	1.32
Apron	.31	.33	.51	.36	.50
Cotton stockings	.31	.32	.28	.33	.29
Silk stockings	1.01	.83	1.04	.70	.87
Part wool stockings	.80	.69	.86	.83	.76
Muslin nightgown	1.03	.81	1.05	.91	.90
Outing flannel nightgown	1.06	.88	1.03	.97	.99
Corset	1.23	1.11	1.80	1.22	1.15
Brassiere	.46	.44	.58	.45	.46
Cotton vest	.32	.31	.31	.27	.29

TABLE 5: AVERAGE MINIMUM RETAIL PRICES OF SELECTED ARTICLES OF WEARING APPAREL, YARD GOODS, CLOTHING ACCESSORIES AND SERVICES IN NEW YORK CITY, 1926—(*Continued*)

Item	Bronx	Brooklyn	Manhattan	Queens	Richmond
Cotton bloomers	$0.61	$0.54	$0.54	$0.55	$0.54
Winter union suit	1.10	.85	1.19	1.09	1.18
Cotton dress slip	1.04	1.11	1.32	1.02	1.04
Crepe kimono	1.04	1.46	1.61	1.71	1.72
Summer hat	3.77	1.91	2.96	2.31	2.74
Winter hat	2.73	1.91	2.91	2.31	2.74
Chamoisette gloves	.86	.63	.79	.79	.84
Wool gloves	.80	.84	.95	.80	.95
House slippers	.78	.74	.77	.77	.82
Oxfords	4.22	3.98	4.75	4.04	3.26
Pumps	4.19	3.98	4.67	4.10	3.26
High shoes	4.63	3.99	5.50	4.95	3.50[a]
Rubbers	1.14	1.07	1.05	1.05	.96
Umbrella	1.00	.98	1.25	1.09	1.25
Handkerchief	.08	.06	.10	.08	.10
Handbag	1.56	.80	1.50	.90	1.00
Clothing for boy, age 12					
Mackinaw	8.33	5.70	6.71	6.56	6.19
Overcoat	10.31	7.77	9.61	8.96	8.12
Two trouser suit	9.61	7.57	9.02	8.93	8.04
Sweater	2.94	2.46	2.71	2.55	2.66
Heavy cotton trousers	1.70	1.27	1.63	1.41	1.46
Shirt	.89	.54	.87	.75	.97
Winter union suit	1.15	.89	.93	.95	1.05
Summer union suit	.72	.52	.54	.54	.70
Night clothes	1.09	.92	1.09	1.06	.99
Wool stockings	.76	.66	.64	.72	.71
Cotton stockings	.28	.30	.31	.29	.29
High shoes	3.26	3.09	3.29	3.27	2.62
Oxfords	3.22	3.07	3.21	3.26	2.59
Sneakers	1.16	1.12	1.33	1.40	1.10
Rubbers	1.07	1.02	1.06	1.08	1.04
Wool gloves	.61	.56	.53	.53	.58
Winter cap	.92	.95	.98	1.08	.90
Summer hat	1.05	.87	.88	1.03	.88
Tie	.42	.33	.34	.38	.38
Belt	.43	.37	.37	.41	.32
Collar	.20	.20	.20	.20	.21
Handkerchief	.07	.07	.09	.08	.08
Clothing for boy, age 2					
Knitted suit	4.56	4.28	4.57	4.85	4.61
Coat	6.74	4.07	4.88	5.98	3.80
Sweater	2.30	1.49	1.78	1.92	2.09
Rompers	.73	.61	.79	.86	.66
Overalls	.62	.50	.62	.61	.53
Summer undershirt	.22	.22	.27	.35	.31
Winter undershirt	.83	.59	.69	.76	.64
Muslin night clothes	.66	.54	.72	.67	.54
Outing flannel night clothes	.71	.57	.75	.85	.62

[a] One quotation only.

TABLE 5: AVERAGE MINIMUM RETAIL PRICES OF SELECTED ARTICLES OF WEARING APPAREL, YARD GOODS, CLOTHING ACCESSORIES AND SERVICES IN NEW YORK CITY, 1926—(*Continued*)

Item	Bronx	Brooklyn	Manhattan	Queens	Richmond
Cotton drawers	$0.38	$0.32	$0.38	$0.44	$0.45
Part wool drawers	.68	.80	.86	.86	.84
Underwaist	.35	.35	.38	.32	.43
Cotton stockings	.28	.23	.25	.24	.25
Cotton socks	.26	.26	.28	.28	.24
High shoes	1.96	1.74	2.24	1.87	1.50
Sandals	1.09	1.02	1.09	1.08	.98
Rubbers	.82	.75	.78	.81	.83
Wool mittens	.43	.33	.40	.40	.45
Winter cap	.76	.75	.86	1.04	.85
Summer hat	.66	.61	.80	.93	.75
Garters	.20	.19	.23	.21	.20
Clothing for girl, age 8					
Coat	6.64	5.22	6.53	6.73	6.03
Sweater	2.66	2.27	2.40	2.72	2.56
Wool dress	3.42	3.02	3.62	3.73	3.62
Cotton dress	1.18	.96	1.46	1.32	1.32
Cotton dress slip	.65	.56	.68	.63	.68
Cotton bloomers	.45	.53	.38	.39	.39
Winter union suit	1.10	.87	.91	1.00	.97
Summer union suit	.78	.51	.57	.58	.62
Night clothes	.67	.59	.69	.83	.61
Underwaist	.39	.37	.39	.34	.40
Wool stockings	.67	.59	.66	.66	.66
Cotton stockings	.32	.28	.28	.28	.28
Oxfords	3.20	2.58	3.04	3.05	2.28
High shoes	3.24	2.78	3.35	3.15	2.24
Sneakers	1.10	1.09	1.18	1.28	1.09
Rubbers	.93	.88	.89	.98	.95
Wool gloves	.58	.54	.51	.55	.55
Winter hat	1.93	1.45	1.69	1.48	1.48
Summer hat	1.75	1.47	1.70	1.63	1.48
Yard goods					
Wool jersey	1.48	1.15	1.66	1.56	1.49
Novelty wool material	1.26	1.10	1.26	1.18	.89
Silk crepe de chine	1.56	1.31	1.57	1.44	1.50
Dress gingham	.24	.23	.23	.23	.22
Apron gingham	.18	.17	.19	.18	.16
Cotton voile	.35	.31	.31	.34	.40
Cotton crepe	.27	.32	.26	.27	.27
Long cloth	.21	.19	.22	.18	.19
Outing flannel	.19	.16	.18	.16	.19
Percale	.22	.23	.24	.19	.22
Sateen	.36	.36	.37	.36	.37
Garter elastic	.08	.13	.11	.12	.10
Cleaning and repairs					
Shoes, half-sole and heel					
Men	1.75	1.65	1.56	1.56	1.75
Women	1.44	1.25	1.31	1.25	1.50
Children	1.30	1.35	1.11	1.15	1.00

Table 5: Average Minimum Retail Prices of Selected Articles of Wearing Apparel, Yard Goods, Clothing Accessories and Services in New York City, 1926—(*Continued*)

Item	Bronx	Brooklyn	Man-hattan	Queens	Rich-mond
Shoes, heel					
Women....................	$0.46	$0.50	$0.44	$0.50	$0.50
Suit, clean and press					
Men......................	1.50	1.69	1.41	1.67	1.50
Women....................	1.70	2.17	1.63	1.92	2.00
Suit, press					
Men......................	.46	.50	.45	.50	.50

Summary

The kinds, quantities and duration of use of clothing for persons or families at any social or occupational level are entirely unstandardized. This is due to the constant shifting in style, fabric and type of garment, as well as to lack of classified data regarding the actual purchases and use of garments. This lack of standardization appears particularly in the case of women's clothing. New budgets were accordingly drawn for the present survey, as a means of measuring the cost of clothing in New York City in 1926. These are designed to represent as far as possible average minimum consumption at a fair American standard of living. They are typical only, however, and it is probable that there could be some shifting of quantities within the cost limits allowed. Prices were secured from the shops which cater to a modest income trade. Averages of these are given for each item for each borough, and the combinations in balanced clothing budgets for one year are given in Chapters VI, VII, VIII and IX.

CHAPTER V

SUNDRIES

IN the list of goods and services grouped as sundries is comprised a large number of miscellaneous items, dissimilar in form and function but together making up a fair share of a normal minimum American standard of living. It is in this group more than in any other that individuals exercise their personal tastes in expenditures and the best that any estimate of minimum requirements can hope to do is to portray a fairly logical distribution, with the understanding that the family which goes to the movies more and reads less, or has heavier demands for church and less for illness or in other ways is forced or prefers to adopt another arrangement of expenditures will redistribute accordingly. Again it should be emphasized that these are only representative or average minimum conditions which, if met, will permit a balanced standard and cost of living; each family will necessarily make its own adjustments from this to suit its own needs.

TRANSPORTATION

The city of New York covers an area of 299 square miles. The business life of the city is so concentrated, however, as to make a few centers the outstanding points of convergence of transportation facilities and to cause serious problems in connection with handling the traffic which flows to and from these points. It is estimated, for example, that more than 131 million passengers left or boarded trains at the Times Square subway stations in 1925; this is an average of about 360,000 persons per day. Grand Central, Penn Station, 14th Street, both east and west side stations, Brooklyn Bridge, Fulton, Cortlandt, Essex and Chambers Streets are all important traffic centers in Manhattan, while in Brooklyn, the Borough Hall, Atlantic Avenue and DeKalb Avenue stations in 1925 each handled traffic averaging over 25 million persons a year. These are all in business districts. Part of the traffic is made up of New York City residents going from one section of the city to another, part of it is connected with rail commutation from outside the city. In 1925, the rapid transit lines alone operated 619.89 miles of track and carried 1,680,800,254 passengers. The surface lines, not including the few routes operated by the city, carried 1,035,977,724 passengers. These two services alone provided 449 rides per capita per year for every man, woman and child living in the city.[1]

In addition, nine municipal ferries, operating exclusively between points within the city, carried over 33 million passengers in 1925;[2] the municipally operated buses are estimated to have carried 40 million and one privately owned bus line reports nearly 68 million passengers carried in 1925.[3] Finally, there is within the city a heavy local traffic on the Long Island, New York Central, New Haven, New York and Westchester, and Staten Island Rapid Transit railroads. In the year ending December 31, 1924, for example, the Long Island reported 443,002 commuters' tickets issued within the city limits; and 7½ million passengers carried almost exclusively within the city, at the so-called "local electric" zone rates; the Staten Island Rapid Transit carried upwards of 12 million passengers wholly within the city limits; the New York Central averaged considerably over 125,000 commuter passengers wholly within the city each month; the New Haven carried 40,000 commuters on its Harlem River Division, and the New York, Westchester and Boston, 1,643,-238,[4] but many of the last two were from outside the city.

The quantity of traveling within the city as shown by these figures is sufficiently impressive, however, to indicate that in any estimate of the cost of living in New York City, a substantial allowance for carfare must be made, even at

[1] There was a total of 1802.71 miles of track operated by the privately owned companies. State of New York, Transit Commission, Summary of Reports of Street Railway Companies . . . for year ended June 30, 1925, p. 25; *ibid.*, Summary of Annual Report, 1925, pp. 57–61.

[2] Figures released by Transit Commission to Newspapers, April 11, 1926.

[3] State of New York, Transit Commission, Summary of Annual Report, 1925, *op. cit.*, pp. 57–61.

[4] *Ibid.*, 1924, pp. 600ff.

the minimum standard. The means by which this transit is made vary, according to the location of the beginning and the end of the journey. To get from the Bronx, or certain parts of Queens to Manhattan or Brooklyn, a subway ride with a five-cent fare will often suffice; sometimes a bus or surface car ride must be added; to get from Manhattan to Brooklyn or vice versa, one fare is usually enough. From Richmond, a five- or an eight-cent ride on the island or commutation costs on the Staten Island Rapid Transit may be added to the five-cent ferry ride across New York Bay and another train ride on subway or elevated may be needed to complete the trip to the other boroughs, at five cents additional cost. In getting around any one of the boroughs itself an expenditure of at least five cents for carfare may be necessary; if transfers or rides on two lines are required, the trip may cost seven or ten cents. In many parts of Queens, there is as yet no subway connection and commutation rates on the Long Island Railroad must considered. Table 6 sum-

TABLE 6: AVERAGE MINIMUM COST OF TRANSPORTATION FROM TYPICAL RESIDENTIAL SECTIONS OF NEW YORK CITY TO SPECIFIED BUSINESS CENTERS OF THE SEPARATE BOROUGHS, 1926

(National Industrial Conference Board)

From—	To Business Center of—				
	Bronx [a]	Brooklyn [b]	Manhattan [c]	Queens [d]	Richmond [e]
Bronx					
East Side	.05	.05	.05	.05	.18
West Side	.05	.05	.05	.05	.18
Brooklyn					
Bushwick	.10	.05	.05	.05	.23
Park Slope—Gowanus	.10	.05	.05	.05	.23
Flatlands	.05	.05	.05	.05	.23
Manhattan					
East Side	.05	.05	.05	.05	.18
West Side	.05	.05	.05	.05	.18
Queens					
Long Island City	.05	.05	.05	.05	.18
Flushing	.11	.11	.11	.06	.24
Jamaica	.10	.05	.05	.05	.23
Richmond					
Stapleton	.18	.18	.18	.18	.08
Port Richmond	.18	.18	.18	.18	.08

[a] 149th St. and 3rd Avenue. [b] Borough Hall.
[c] 42nd Street, Grand Central or Times Square.
[d] Long Island City. [e] Stapleton or Port Richmond.

marizes representative transportation costs in New York City in the spring of 1926. The estimates are necessarily arbitrary, but their basis is given and they are believed to be as representative as any single set of figures can be.

From this table it is possible to estimate the average weekly cost of transportation to work, six days a week, and this is summarized below:

Bronx	$0.60
Brooklyn	.60
Manhattan	.60
Queens	.90
Richmond	2.16[a]

[a] For those residents of Richmond who work on the island the minimum carfare would average only 96 cents a week; on the other hand, for those on the south shore who travel by train to the ferry to go to the other boroughs, the commutation fare in some instances is more than the 8-cent surface carfare.

These figures are based on round trip cost, at the usual rate of fare, except in Queens, where it is assumed that more double fares would be paid. In view of the fact that necessarily some workers in each borough must pay two fares, or pay for transfers, but that, on the other hand, some walk to the places of their employment, at least one way, the estimate seems as satisfactory as any single figure can be.

Carfare is required for recreation, shopping, church, school, in varying amounts in the separate boroughs and parts of boroughs. Some neighborhoods are still so sparsely settled as not to support theatres, or stores carrying anything but staple necessities; in others, every requirement for minimum living may be satisfied, with such excursions beyond the confines of the neighborhood as taste and preference rather than necessity dictate. It is probable, however, that carfare requirements pretty well even up in the course of a year, for while residents of the more sparsely settled sections may need to pay carfare in connection with shopping or attending the movies, they have many opportunities at hand for recreation which require no expenditures whatever. The dweller in districts thickly enough settled to support large shops and theatres on the other hand requires carfare to go to the parks, beaches and for country outings. For example, the resident of Stapleton for a five- or an eight-cent fare can reach some of the finest bathing beaches in the city and, without carfare at all, can find ample picnic grounds for Sunday diversions; for his more extensive shopping he comes to Manhattan. The resident of Bushwick finds every necessity gratified within his own neighborhood, but to go to the beach or open country requires at least a five-cent fare. An average of 10 cents per person per week in the Bronx, Brooklyn and Manhattan, 15 cents in Queens and 18 cents in Richmond is, therefore, allowed in each family to take care of necessary transportation, in addition to carfare to work.

Recreation

Recreation in New York City is plentiful and cheap. Dozens of community centers, employees' associations maintained in the different business establishments, churches, lodges and clubs provide opportunity for social intercourse; motion picture theatres abound in nearly every neighborhood; cheap transportation provides pleasure in itself in the summer or affords easy means of reaching the numerous parks, playgrounds and beaches. There are swimming pools, gymnasiums, libraries, free concerts. No one in New York City should lack for healthful and satisfactory recreation at small cost, if only he is directed to it.

Probably the most popular single source of amusement at the present time is the motion picture theatre. In the spring of 1926, admission charges at the neighborhood houses varied from 5 cents for children at week-day matinees to one dollar for adults at evening performances. While the prices collected in the present survey differed a little from borough to borough, this was probably more chance of sample than actual difference in cost of attending the same type of entertainment. An allowance of 20 cents per week for each adult and 15 cents for each child would appear to be a sufficient minimum allowance for recreation. If this by choice were spent for bus rides, trips to the beach or parks, the same purpose would be served.

Reading Material, Stationery, Postage, Telephone, Etc.

New York City is well supplied with free public libraries, having branches conveniently located all over the city, which are extensively patronized. The figures showing book circulation alone indicate that in 1925, 9,018,339 books were taken for home use in Manhattan, the Bronx and Richmond, 5,500,000 in Brooklyn and 1,976,566 in Queens.

There are over 60 newspapers published on a daily or a weekly basis in the five boroughs of New York City. A number of these are foreign language papers; others are exclusively local sheets, while a few are great metropolitan dailies. In the spring of 1926 these sold for two or three cents on week-days and for five or ten cents on Sundays.

Telephones are coming into constantly increasing use, there being over a million in operation in the city, with more than ten million calls coming in and going out per day, but as yet they are not generally found in the homes of families living at a minimum American standard. Every one, however, has occasion at some time or other for a telephone call at the corner drug or grocery store; and, though correspondence may be limited among industrial and office workers at a minimum standard of living, some allowance for postage, stationery and the like is necessary. Among the million school children in the city some expenditures for equipment are required. The allowance for this group of items is intended to supply a daily paper and a small amount extra to cover the needs noted above. As most of this expenditure would be required by adults, it has been made the same for all families, no matter what their size.

Medical Care and Sick Benefits

Health supervision and medical care are likewise ample in New York City. From pre-natal clinics to homes for incurables, resources are available at small cost to those who are in need. The health of school children is supervised; many of the industries have medical departments to watch over the welfare of their employees; nursing service at cost, or less, or free to insurance policy holders, as well as all of the free resources of the hospitals and clinics in a great city provide for the health of New York City's population. Nor is this necessarily on a charity basis. Public health work has gone far toward reducing the New York City death rate to

12.2 per thousand population, and the infant mortality rate to 64.2 per thousand births.[1]

People who become ill must have care, however, and should pay for such attention as they receive. Doctors' fees among the people studied in this investigation varied slightly but enough of them charged $2 for an office visit and $3 for a house call to make those rates standard. In a fair minimum budget, only the simplest provision for such service can be made, but an allowance of 20 cents a week per person in an average family would pay for ordinary care of health, including teeth, eyes and occasional special attention, in the spring of 1926. With the free health insurance provided in the mutual benefit associations of many of the industries, this allowance would also provide for a minimum rate of sick benefits taken out by many working men.

Insurance

The custom of carrying life insurance is well established among New York's wage earning population. Among the lowlier folk this takes the form of industrial policies, for which payment is made to collectors from the issuing companies each week; among those who can arrange to pay on a quarterly basis, straight life insurance is carried. The wife and children in families whose chief wage earner is thus insured are almost certain to be insured also to cover the cost of their funerals.

Agents of the insurance companies estimated differently the quantity carried. In one Manhattan district, $1.50 per family per week was said to be spent for life insurance. This was confirmed by agents of another company in the Bronx who put the average weekly outlay somewhere between $1.30 and $1.50; still another agent in the Bronx said $2.50 a week was spent for insurance on the man's life alone; and another thought 70 cents a week would carry the family cost of industrial insurance. The number carrying insurance was estimated at anywhere from 65% to 90% of the industrial population. Among some of the social welfare agencies there is a feeling that the amount spent for insurance, which

[1] United States, Treasury Department, *Public Health Reports*, June 11, 1926, p. 1174.

is primarily designed to provide a costly funeral, is often beyond the means of the families thus insured.

In addition to the life insurance issued by the commercial companies, fraternal organizations having benefits as well as social features are very popular with certain sections of the population. Many of the large industrial concerns in the city also insure their employees on a group plan, providing death benefits of a thousand dollars or more. These are not to be relied on as the only source of benefit, however, since termination of employment cancels the protection or throws continuation of the policy back on the individual at higher rates.

The usual minimum insurance held to be proper by social welfare organizations in the city in the spring of 1926 was 25 cents a week for each adult and 10 cents for each child. This would provide for the cost of burial when needed. For a small addition to this amount, a thousand dollar straight life policy might be purchased. It is said that a thousand dollar endowment policy, at still a little more a week, is a popular form of saving among young office workers.

Organizations

In addition to lodges and fraternal organizations, many wage earners and members of their families belong to societies of various kinds for which dues and assessments are required. The employees' organizations in the different industrial establishments, church, neighborhood or labor organizations, each demands a small outlay of some kind. Even the children need a few pennies for club or scout troup. This may all be regarded as in addition to the allowance previously considered for health or recreation, and while minimum standard families can scarcely be thought of as belonging to many organizations they probably require a small outlay for one such item. Although considerable new data were collected on this subject it is necessarily of a heterogeneous character and provides little by way of exact basis for estimating how much a minimum allowance for such purposes should be. The amount given in addition to the allowances on other items, such as recreation and insurance, was enough for average minimum requirements in the spring of 1926.

Church, Charity and Gifts

So, also, allowances must be made, even at a minimum standard of living, for contributions to church and charity, for the payment of incidental costs, if not actual tuition or outlay for books, for the children attending church schools, for gifts to the children at Christmas.[1] There are no set rules about this; the sums allowed would enable minimum standard families to contribute their fair share in drives, for the support of the church, and to meet other incidental demands noted above.

Candy, Tobacco, Etc.

Men will smoke and children will have their candy, no matter what the standard of living. The allowance made for this item, on the basis of approximately two packages of popular price cigarettes per week and an equal expenditure by the other members of the family, is apparently a reasonable minimum. The allowance for sweets is in addition to that provided in the food budget.

Cleaning Supplies and Toilet Requisites

Soap, tooth paste, a few simple household remedies, razor blades, tooth brushes, hair cuts for all of the family these days, as well as household supplies for kitchen, laundry and bathroom, require a considerable outlay when totalled for a year. If the services of a wet wash or rough dry laundry are included, the cost is even greater.

Furniture and Furnishings

Furniture and furnishings are as much unstandardized as is clothing. There are data regarding average use[2] but none regarding adequacy. Students of the problem have,

[1] No allowance has been made for gifts among adults, the thought being of a mutual exchange in which costs would cancel; no allowance is made for entertainment at home or meals offered to guests, for the same reason.

[2] United States Bureau of Labor Statistics, Bulletin No. 357, *op. cit.*, pp. 392–401.

however, worked out on more or less theoretical bases expenditures necessary for furnishing certain types of rooms with certain types of furniture.[1] These have been suggestive for the present survey.

In determining the outlay necessary for the replacement of furniture, rugs, draperies, bed and table linen, and other household equipment, it is assumed that only the ordinary wear and tear will be considered and that no large purchases will have to be financed. Average replacement under these conditions has been estimated at 6% of the current cost;[2] another student placed the depreciation of linen, bedding and towels, kitchenware and silverware at 7% and that of furniture at 4%.[3] This works out at a weighted average of about 6%, and for all practical purposes this figure may be adopted.

Referring to the minimum budgets noted in footnote one on this page it appears that initial equipment for an apartment consisting of two bedrooms, a living room, kitchen, hall and bath, at prices current in 1926, can be obtained for a minimum outlay of approximately $600. To the 6% of this necessarily spent for upkeep and replacement may be added a few dollars for an occasional tool, electric light bulbs and other odds and ends always needed around a house but difficult to itemize.

These prices would not permit of very extensive buying on deferred payment plans which materially increase the cash price cost,[4] but it is thought that the usual annual outlay contemplated would not require elaborate financing.

Summary

While the goods and services listed in this chapter as sundries comprise a large list, they are with few exceptions

[1] R. H. Macy & Co., "Furnishing Your Home On a Budget," New York, 1924; John Wanamaker, "Home Budget Service," Seventh Edition, New York, 1925; Abraham and Straus, Inc., "Practical Home Planning," Brooklyn, 1925.

[2] United States Bureau of Labor Statistics, "Tentative Quantity and Cost Budget," *op. cit.*, p. 39.

[3] California State Civil Service Commission, Cost of Living Survey, Report, *op. cit.*, pp. 41, 57, 71.

[4] At many of the furniture stores there is a difference of 10% or more between cash and credit prices; at the department stores which sell furniture on the basis of deferred payments the carrying charge, if there is any at all, is usually not so great.

without standardization as to quantity or use. The allowances in most instances must be estimates. The bases of these are given, however, and they may be readjusted in any reasonable manner to meet other needs. A fair average distribution among families of different sizes and for families and individuals of varying occupation is given in Chapters VI, VII, VIII, and IX.

PART II: THE COST OF LIVING OF INDUSTRIAL WORKERS

CHART 1: AVERAGE MINIMUM COST PER WEEK OF MAINTAINING A FAIR AMERICAN STANDARD OF LIVING FOR THE FAMILY OF AN INDUSTRIAL WORKER IN NEW YORK CITY, 1926

Based on figures in Table 13 and Table 27

(National Industrial Conference Board)

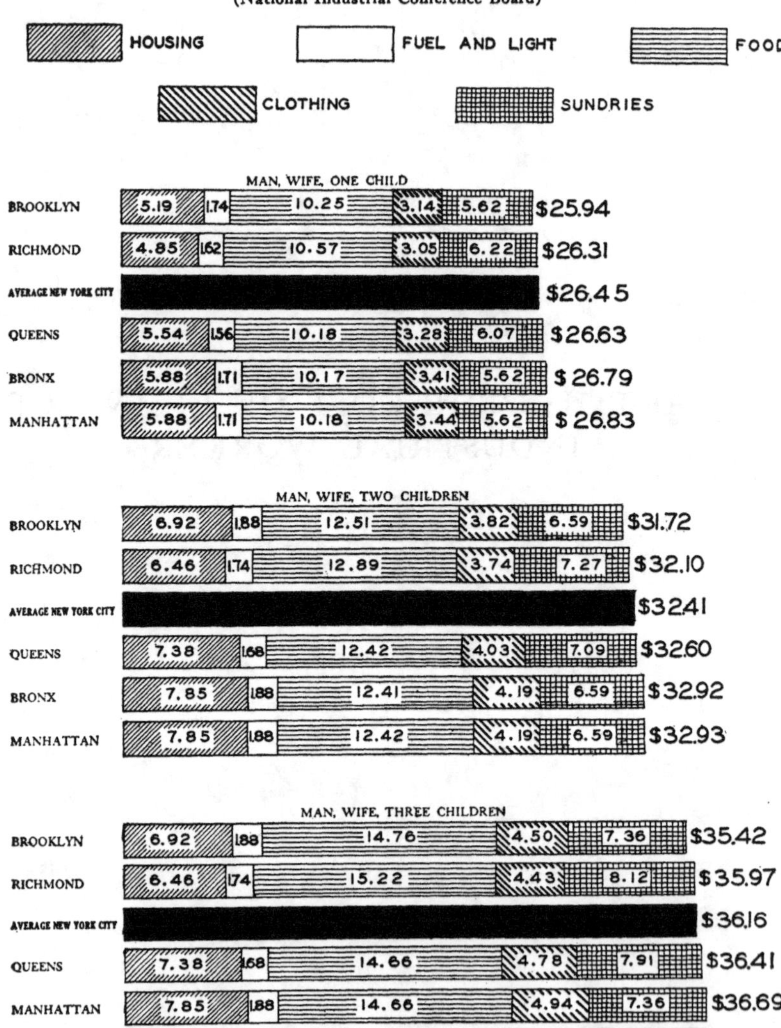

CHAPTER VI

COST OF LIVING FOR FAMILIES

THE data from which the average minimum cost of maintaining a fair American standard of living may be estimated were given in the preceding chapters. These consist of a specific list of goods and services selected so as to indicate representative minimum consumption, and their cost at prices prevailing in the spring of 1926. It should be clearly understood that both the consumption data and the price data are averages, representative of conditions in general but not necessarily indicative of the situation as it confronts any particular family.

Housing

The housing of minimum standard industrial workers in New York City is to be found in unheated apartments, or, in the newer boroughs, possibly in small houses where the tenant furnishes his own heat. The generally accepted minimum space required to care for groups of persons living together, without overcrowding, is one and one-half persons per room. With the housing situation what it is at the present time in New York City, and the prevailing level of rents, it is possible that actual conditions more nearly approach the theoretical than in many years, although extremely poor families constantly on the poverty line in the past have got along with this minimum space or even less. For the most part, however, this ratio is reached if at all by the larger family groups. A relief organization in Brooklyn, for example, in 1924 found among families under its care an average of 5.3 persons per family, with an average of 1.4 persons per room; a similar organization in Manhattan in 1925 found an average of 5.1 persons in 3.2 rooms, or 1.6 persons per room. These ratios are higher than those shown by the other records made availlabe in the present survey. Among a group of 132 married employees in one department of a large Brooklyn industrial establishment, there was an average of at least one room per person, even among the lowest paid employees. In no case, however, did the average family approach four persons. Age and sex make some difference in the space required, and families with several small children but only two adults may possibly do with fewer rooms than where the need for more privacy must be considered. From the above, the following may be estimated as the minimum requirements for housing in New York City in 1926:

Man, wife and one child	3 rooms and bath
Man, wife and two children	4 rooms and bath
Man, wife and three children	4 rooms and bath

In the present survey, in determining the outlay necessary for rent each year, the rent per room has been multiplied by the number of rooms required per family. This was done in recognition of the fact that accommodations are not everywhere available in exactly the size units always required, but with the assumption that places which are too large will return at least the cost of the surplus space through income from older children or other lodgers, so that the outlay necessary for rent by the male head of a dependent family is only for that portion of the house or apartment which is actually occupied by such family. The average minimum cost of housing as thus estimated for families of different size at rents prevailing in the spring of 1926, is summarized in Table 7. It cannot be too strongly emphasized that the figures given do not refer necessarily to identical housing in the separate places, since comparable accommodations are often not to be found. Rather, they refer to the prevailing type of housing occupied by industrial workers in the localities specified.

These figures are perhaps somewhat above the minimum level of rents being paid by families of industrial workers in New York City in the spring of 1926. This is due to the fact that they include payment for a bath room, which is lacking in many low price apartments at the present time, especially in Manhattan; it is due, also, to the fact that they are the rents being charged new tenants going into the premises described, and are not necessarily the rents prevailing as the average level in any house. There is no doubt that a move of domicile tends to increase the outlay necessary for housing, whether the movement is within a given locality or whether it is from one section of the city to another.

TABLE 7: AVERAGE MINIMUM OUTLAY NECESSARY FOR HOUSING FOR ONE MONTH AND FOR ONE YEAR FOR THE FAMILY OF AN INDUSTRIAL WORKER LIVING AT A FAIR AMERICAN STANDARD IN NEW YORK CITY, 1926[a]

(National Industrial Conference Board)

Family of Man, Wife and—	Bronx	Brooklyn	Manhattan	Queens	Richmond
			Monthly Cost		
(Average rent per room)...	$8.50	$7.50	$8.50	$8.00	$7.00
One child................	25.50	22.50	25.50	25.00	21.00
Two children.............	34.00	30.00	34.00	32.00	28.00
Three children...........	34.00	30.00	34.00	32.00	28.00
			Yearly Cost		
One child................	306.00	270.00	306.00	288.00	252.00
Two children.............	408.00	360.00	408.00	384.00	336.00
Three children...........	408.00	360.00	408.00	384.00	336.00

[a] These are for customary, not necessarily for identical, accommodations.

FUEL AND LIGHT

The quantity of fuel and light required to meet the needs of a fair minimum American standard of living depends entirely on the character of the housing to be heated and lighted. This includes not only the number of rooms but also their relative exposure, heating medium and layout. In the old "railroad" apartments, found in all boroughs, where one room opens directly out of another, warmth is furnished from the range in the kitchen and possibly a heater of some kind in another room. In the frame houses and apartments with furnaces in the cellars, more fuel is required, because of the greater exposure and often because the layout of the rooms is such as to require more piping.

In Chapter II the basic data were given for estimating the cost of coal, kerosene, gas, electricity and other heat and light services. Assuming that industrial workers' families in all of the boroughs of New York City live in apartments which they themselves must heat, the average minimum cost of this, combined with the average minimum outlay necessary for gas and electricity per year, at prices current in the spring of 1926, is summarized in Table 8.

TABLE 8: AVERAGE MINIMUM COST OF FUEL AND LIGHT FOR ONE YEAR FOR THE FAMILY OF AN INDUSTRIAL WORKER LIVING AT A FAIR AMERICAN STANDARD IN NEW YORK CITY, 1926

(National Industrial Conference Board)

Family of Man, Wife and—	Bronx	Brooklyn	Manhattan	Queens	Richmond
One child[a]	$89.08	$90.28	$89.08	$81.10	$84.10
Two children[b]	97.70	97.70	97.70	87.50	90.50
Three children[b]	97.70	97.70	97.70	87.50	90.50

[a] Three rooms. [b] Four rooms.

FOOD

The food allowance given in Table 4 showed the average minimum quantity required for one week for a family of four adults and one older or two younger children, living at a fair American standard in New York City in 1926. These quantities, multiplied by the average price of each article, give the average minimum weekly cost. Of this total it was found that the man at moderately heavy work required 22.65%; the woman at work in the home, 20.39%; the man and the woman at light work, 20.39% and 18.35% respectively; the older boy, or the two younger children, required 18.22%. From these data the average minimum weekly cost of each one's share of the food consumed was calculated. By adding together the cost of the food for persons of specific ages, sex and occupation, as shown in Table 4, the cost of food for any given type of family may be found.

For industrial workers' families of different sizes, living at a fair American standard in New York City, the average minimum cost of food for one week and for one year, based on prices being charged in the spring of 1926, is given in Table 9. The cost of food for one child was estimated to be one-third the average for one older and two younger children, as shown in Table 4.

TABLE 9: AVERAGE MINIMUM COST OF FOOD FOR ONE WEEK AND FOR ONE YEAR FOR THE FAMILY OF AN INDUSTRIAL WORKER LIVING AT A FAIR AMERICAN STANDARD IN NEW YORK CITY, 1926

(National Industrial Conference Board)

Family of Man, Wife and—	Bronx	Brooklyn	Manhattan	Queens	Richmond
			Weekly Cost		
One child	$10.17	$10.25	$10.18	$10.18	$10.57
Two children	12.41	12.51	12.42	12.42	12.89
Three children	14.65	14.76	14.66	14.66	15.22
			Yearly Cost		
One child	$528.84	$533.00	$529.36	$529.36	$549.64
Two children	645.32	650.52	645.84	645.84	670.28
Three children	761.80	767.52	762.32	762.32	791.44

In apportioning the cost of a family's food, it may fairly be presumed, as already pointed out, that the older boy or girl pays his or her own way, so that all the father is responsible for is the cost of food for himself, his wife and the younger children. In pro-rating this, there is necessarily a certain element of error due to the fact that if the family included several small children the food purchased would differ somewhat from that used where there were more adults. On the whole, however, it is probable that the difference in cost is not so great as seriously to affect the results and that the cost worked out on the calorie needs for different types of families is sufficiently accurate for all practical purposes. Nor does it appear that any extra allowance needs to be made for the fact that for the most part industrial workers in New York City do not go home for the mid-day meal, but carry their lunch with them instead of buying restaurant food. With the allowance given there is, apparently, ample provision for any extra cost involved in the way of supplying food suitable to be carried in a lunch box.

CLOTHING

The budgets used to measure the minimum cost of clothing for an industrial worker and his family living at a fair American standard in New York City in 1926 were the same in all boroughs. They were based on the assumption that the

TABLE 10A: AVERAGE MINIMUM COST OF CLOTHING FOR ONE YEAR FOR A MARRIED MALE INDUSTRIAL WORKER LIVING AT A FAIR AMERICAN STANDARD IN NEW YORK CITY, 1926

(National Industrial Conference Board)

Item	Quantity Allowance	Bronx		Brooklyn		Manhattan		Queens		Richmond	
		Average Price	Yearly Cost	Average Price	Yearly Cost	Average Price	Yearly Cost	Average Price	Yearly Cost	Average Price	Yearly Cost
Suit	⅔	$19.91	$13.27	$19.62	$13.08	$19.73	$13.15	$20.40	$13.60	$16.45	$10.97
Overcoat	¼	18.90	4.73	19.33	4.83	21.32	5.33	21.42	5.36	21.05	5.26
Extra trousers	1	3.42	3.42	3.88	3.88	3.86	3.86	3.14	3.14	3.37	3.37
Sweater	1	4.16	4.16	3.59	3.59	3.85	3.85	3.32	3.32	2.83	2.83
Madras shirt	2	1.41	2.82	1.47	2.94	1.54	3.08	1.47	2.94	1.45	2.90
Cotton work shirt	2	.97	1.94	.95	1.90	.95	1.90	.94	1.88	.94	1.88
Wool work shirt	1	1.99	1.99	1.93	1.93	2.22	2.22	2.01	2.01	2.04	2.04
Overalls	3	2.73	8.19	3.02	9.06	2.89	8.67	2.92	8.76	2.42	7.26
Oxfords	½	4.76	2.38	4.73	2.37	4.84	2.42	4.58	2.29	3.77	1.89
High shoes	½	4.77	2.39	4.82	2.41	5.07	2.54	4.48	2.24	3.65	1.83
Work shoes	1	4.39	4.39	4.13	4.13	4.30	4.30	3.94	3.94	2.41	2.41
Rubbers	½	1.36	.68	1.35	.68	1.36	.68	1.32	.66	1.35	.68
Wool socks	4	.45	1.80	.41	1.64	.45	1.80	.42	1.68	.42	1.68
Cotton socks	4	.23	.92	.22	.88	.22	.88	.19	.76	.21	.84
Summer union suit	2	1.17	2.34	.99	1.98	1.03	2.06	.98	1.96	.92	1.84
Winter union suit	1	1.48	1.48	1.46	1.46	1.48	1.48	1.49	1.49	1.48	1.48
Night clothes	2	1.43	2.86	1.42	2.84	1.37	2.74	1.33	2.66	1.38	2.76
Felt hat	½	3.42	1.71	3.03	1.52	2.96	1.48	3.41	1.71	3.29	1.65
Straw hat	½	2.19	1.10	1.80	.90	1.96	.88	1.74	.87	1.80	.90
Cap	1	1.39	1.39	1.23	1.23	1.06	1.06	1.26	1.26	1.10	1.10
Wool gloves	½	.94	.47	.88	.44	.86	.43	.84	.42	.87	.44
Work gloves	3	.14	.42	.15	.45	.19	.57	.20	.60	.18	.54
Collar	4	.20	.80	.19	.76	.19	.76	.20	.80	.21	.84
Tie	3	.70	2.10	.62	1.86	.73	2.19	.58	1.74	.52	1.56
Garters	2	.26	.52	.25	.50	.28	.56	.25	.50	.24	.48
Belt	⅓	.57	.19	.62	.21	.65	.22	.51	.17	.47	.16
Suspenders	1	.52	.52	.49	.49	.53	.53	.47	.47	.46	.46
White handkerchief	4	.10	.40	.09	.36	.10	.40	.09	.36	.10	.40
Colored handkerchief	2	.15	.30	.14	.28	.13	.26	.12	.24	.10	.20
Umbrella	¼	1.44	.36	1.19	.30	1.27	.32	1.05	.26	1.25	.31
Half-soles and heels	2	1.75	3.50	1.65	3.30	1.56	3.12	1.56	3.12	1.75	3.50
Cleaning and pressing suit	1	1.50	1.50	1.69	1.69	1.41	1.41	1.67	1.67	1.50	1.50
Pressing suit	1	.46	.46	.50	.50	.45	.45	.50	.50	.50	.50
Incidentals			1.00		1.00		1.00		1.00		1.00
Total			$76.50		$75.39		$76.70		$74.38		$67.46

TABLE 10[illegible]. AVERAGE MINIMUM COST OF CLOTHING FOR ONE YEAR FOR THE WIFE OF AN INDUSTRIAL WORKER LIVING AT A FAIR AMERICAN STANDARD IN NEW YORK CITY, 1926

(National Industrial Conference Board)

Item	Quantity Allowance	Bronx		Brooklyn		Manhattan		Queens		Richmond	
		Average Price	Yearly Cost	Average Price	Yearly Cost	Average Price	Yearly Cost	Average Price	Yearly Cost	Average Price	Yearly Cost
Coat	½	$13.06	$6.53	$10.50	$5.25	$14.90	$7.45	$13.67	$6.84	$11.25	$5.63
Sweater	½	3.15	1.58	2.30	1.15	3.30	1.65	3.68	1.84	2.32	1.16
Wool dress	½[a]	4.66	2.33	3.84	1.92	5.10	2.55	4.86	2.43	4.68	2.34
Silk dress	½[a]	7.20	3.60	6.20	3.10	7.24	3.62	6.72	3.36	6.96	3.48
Gingham dress	1 [a]	1.21	1.21	1.17	1.17	1.17	1.17	1.17	1.17	1.13	1.13
Voile dress	1 [a]	1.65	1.65	1.49	1.49	1.49	1.49	1.61	1.61	1.85	1.85
House dress	2 [a]	.76	1.52	.79	1.58	.82	1.64	.67	1.34	.76	1.52
Apron[b]	3 [a]	.28	.86	.27	.82	.30	.91	.28	.86	.25	.77
Cotton stockings	3	.31	.93	.32	.96	.28	.84	.33	.99	.29	.87
Wool stockings	2	.80	1.60	.69	1.38	.86	1.72	.83	1.66	.76	1.52
Silk stockings	1	1.01	1.01	.83	.83	1.04	1.04	.70	.70	.87	.87
Muslin nightgown	1	1.03	1.03	.81	.81	1.05	1.05	.91	.91	.90	.90
Outing flannel nightgown	1	1.06	1.06	.88	.88	1.03	1.03	.97	.97	.99	.99
Corset	2	1.23	2.46	1.11	2.22	1.80	3.60	1.22	2.44	1.15	2.30
Brassiere	2	.46	.92	.44	.88	.58	1.16	.45	.90	.46	.92
Cotton vest	2	.32	.64	.31	.62	.31	.62	.27	.54	.29	.58
Cotton bloomers	3	.61	1.83	.54	1.62	.54	1.62	.55	1.65	.54	1.62
Winter union suit	2	1.10	2.20	.85	1.70	1.19	2.38	1.09	2.18	1.18	2.36
Sateen dress slip	1	1.04	1.04	1.11	1.11	1.32	1.32	1.02	1.02	1.04	1.04
Cotton crepe kimono	¼[a]	1.08	.27	1.28	.32	1.04	.26	1.08	.27	1.08	.27
Summer hat	1	3.77	3.77	1.91	1.91	2.96	2.96	2.31	2.31	2.74	2.74
Winter hat	½	2.73	1.37	1.91	.96	2.91	1.46	2.31	1.16	2.74	1.37
Chamoisette gloves	½	.86	.43	.63	.32	.79	.40	.79	.40	.84	.42
Wool gloves	½	.80	.40	.84	.42	.95	.48	.80	.40	.95	.48
Felt house slippers	⅓	.78	.26	.74	.25	.77	.26	.77	.26	.82	.27
Oxfords	1	4.22	4.22	3.98	3.98	4.75	4.75	4.04	4.04	3.26	3.26
Pumps	1	4.19	4.19	3.98	3.98	4.67	4.67	4.10	4.10	3.26	3.26
Rubbers	½	1.14	.57	1.07	.54	1.05	.53	1.05	.53	.96	.48
Umbrella	¼	1.00	.25	.98	.25	1.25	.31	1.09	.27	1.25	.31
Handkerchief	6	.08	.48	.06	.36	.10	.60	.08	.48	.10	.60
Handbag	⅓	1.56	.52	.80	.27	1.50	.50	.90	.30	1.00	.33
Cleaning and pressing	1	1.70	1.70	2.17	2.17	1.63	1.63	1.92	1.92	2.00	2.00
Half-soles and heels	1½	1.44	2.16	1.25	1.88	1.31	1.97	1.25	1.88	1.50	2.25
Heels	1	.46	.46	.50	.50	.44	.44	.50	.50	.50	.50
Incidentals			5.00		5.00		5.00		5.00		5.00
Total			$60.05		$52.60		$63.08		$57.23		$55.39

[a] Material of which garments are made.

[b] The price of one apron was calculated from the cost of three.

TABLE 10C: AVERAGE MINIMUM COST OF CLOTHING FOR ONE YEAR FOR THE 12-YEAR-OLD SON OF AN INDUSTRIAL WORKER LIVING AT A FAIR AMERICAN STANDARD IN NEW YORK CITY, 1926
(National Industrial Conference Board)

Item	Quantity Allowance	Bronx		Brooklyn		Manhattan		Queens		Richmond	
		Average Price	Yearly Cost	Average Price	Yearly Cost	Average Price	Yearly Cost	Average Price	Yearly Cost	Average Price	Yearly Cost
Mackinaw	½	$8.33	$4.17	$5.70	$2.85	$6.71	$3.36	$6.56	$3.28	$6.19	$3.10
Sweater	½	2.94	1.47	2.46	1.23	2.71	1.36	2.55	1.28	2.66	1.33
Two-trouser suit	1	9.61	9.61	7.57	7.57	9.02	9.02	8.93	8.93	8.04	8.04
Heavy cotton trousers	2	1.70	3.40	1.27	2.54	1.63	3.26	1.41	2.82	1.46	2.92
Shirt or blouse	4	.89	3.56	.54	2.16	.87	3.48	.75	3.00	.97	3.88
Winter union suit	2	1.15	2.30	.89	1.78	.93	1.86	.95	1.90	1.05	2.10
Summer union suit	2	.72	1.44	.52	1.04	.54	1.08	.54	1.08	.70	1.40
Night clothes	2	1.09	2.18	.92	1.84	1.09	2.18	1.06	2.12	.99	1.98
Wool stockings	2	.76	1.52	.66	1.32	.64	1.28	.72	1.44	.71	1.42
Cotton stockings	8	.28	2.24	.30	2.40	.31	2.48	.29	2.32	.29	2.32
Oxfords	1	3.22	3.22	3.07	3.07	3.21	3.21	3.26	3.26	2.59	2.59
Sneakers	1	1.16	1.16	1.12	1.12	1.33	1.33	1.40	1.40	1.10	1.10
High shoes	2	3.26	6.52	3.09	6.18	3.29	6.58	3.27	6.54	2.62	5.24
Rubbers	1	1.07	1.07	1.02	1.02	1.06	1.06	1.08	1.08	1.04	1.04
Wool gloves	1	.61	.61	.56	.56	.53	.53	.53	.53	.58	.58
Winter cap	1	.92	.92	.95	.95	.98	.98	1.08	1.08	.90	.90
Summer hat	1	1.05	1.05	.87	.87	.88	.88	1.03	1.03	.88	.88
Necktie	2	.42	.84	.33	.66	.34	.68	.38	.76	.38	.76
Cotton handkerchief	6	.07	.42	.07	.42	.09	.54	.08	.48	.08	.48
Belt	½	.43	22	.37	.19	.37	.19	.41	.21	.32	.16
Garters	2 [a]	.08	.16	.13	.26	.11	.22	.12	.24	.10	.20
Half-soles and heels	3	1.30	3.90	1.35	4.05	1.11	3.33	1.15	3.45	1.00	3.00
Incidentals			.50		.50		.50		.50		.50
Total			$52.48		$44.58		$49.39		$48.73		$45.92

[a] Material of which they are made.

Table 10d: Average Minimum Cost of Clothing for One Year for the 8-Year-Old Daughter of an Industrial Worker Living at a Fair American Standard in New York City, 1926

(National Industrial Conference Board)

Item	Quantity Allowance	Bronx		Brooklyn		Manhattan		Queens		Richmond	
		Average Price	Yearly Cost	Average Price	Yearly Cost	Average Price	Yearly Cost	Average Price	Yearly Cost	Average Price	Yearly Cost
Coat	½	$6.64	$3.32	$5.22	$2.61	$6.53	$3.27	$6.73	$3.37	$6.03	$3.02
Sweater	½	2.66	1.33	2.27	1.14	2.40	1.20	2.72	1.36	2.56	1.28
Wool dress (with bloomers)	1 [a]	2.72	2.72	2.23	2.23	2.99	2.99	2.84	2.84	2.74	2.74
Gingham dress (with bloomers)	2 [a]	.92	1.84	.89	1.78	.89	1.78	.89	1.78	.86	1.72
Voile dress (with slip)	1 [a]	1.25	1.25	1.13	1.13	1.13	1.13	1.22	1.22	1.40	1.40
Bloomers	3	.45	1.35	.53	1.59	.38	1.14	.39	1.17	.39	1.17
Winter union suit	2	1.10	2.20	.87	1.74	.91	1.82	1.00	2.00	.97	1.94
Summer union suit	2	.78	1.56	.51	1.02	.57	1.14	.58	1.16	.62	1.24
Night clothes	2	.67	1.34	.59	1.18	.69	1.38	.83	1.66	.61	1.22
Underwaist	3	.39	1.17	.37	1.11	.39	1.17	.34	1.02	.40	1.20
Wool stockings	2	.67	1.34	.59	1.18	.66	1.32	.66	1.32	.66	1.32
Cotton stockings	5	.32	1.60	.28	1.40	.28	1.40	.28	1.40	.28	1.40
Oxfords	1	.20	3.20	2.58	2.58	3.04	3.04	3.05	3.05	2.28	2.28
Sneakers	1	1.10	1.10	1.09	1.09	1.18	1.18	1.28	1.28	1.09	1.09
High shoes	2	3.24	6.48	2.78	5.56	3.35	6.70	3.15	6.30	2.24	4.48
Rubbers	1	.93	.93	.88	.88	.89	.89	.98	.98	.95	.95
Wool gloves	1	.58	.58	.54	.54	.51	.51	.55	.55	.55	.55
Winter hat	1	1.93	1.93	1.45	1.45	1.69	1.69	1.48	1.48	1.48	1.48
Summer hat	1	1.75	1.75	1.47	1.47	1.70	1.70	1.63	1.63	1.48	1.48
Handkerchief	6	.08	.48	.06	.36	.10	.60	.08	.48	.10	.60
Garters	2 [a]	.08	.16	.13	.26	.11	.22	.12	.24	.10	.20
Half-soles and heels	3	1.30	3.90	1.35	4.05	1.11	3.33	1.15	3.45	1.00	3.00
Incidentals			.50		.50		.50		.50		.50
Total			$42.03		$36.85		$40.10		$40.24		$36.26

[a] Material of which they are made.

TABLE 10E: AVERAGE MINIMUM COST OF CLOTHING FOR ONE YEAR FOR THE 2-YEAR-OLD SON OF AN INDUSTRIAL WORKER LIVING AT A FAIR AMERICAN STANDARD IN NEW YORK CITY, 1926

(National Industrial Conference Board)

Item	Quantity Allowance	Bronx		Brooklyn		Manhattan		Queens		Richmond	
		Average Price	Yearly Cost	Average Price	Yearly Cost	Average Price	Yearly Cost	Average Price	Yearly Cost	Average Price	Yearly Cost
Knitted suit	½	$4.56	$2.28	$4.28	$2.14	$4.57	$2.29	$4.85	$2.43	$4.61	$2.31
Sweater	½	2.30	1.15	1.49	.75	1.78	.89	1.92	.96	2.09	1.05
Rompers	3	.73	2.19	.61	1.83	.79	2.37	.86	2.58	.66	1.98
Overalls	3	.62	1.86	.50	1.50	.62	1.86	.61	1.83	.53	1.59
Summer undershirt	2	.22	.44	.22	.44	.27	.54	.35	.70	.31	.62
Winter undershirt	2	.83	1.66	.59	1.18	.69	1.38	.76	1.52	.64	1.28
Muslin night clothes	1	.66	.66	.54	.54	.72	.72	.67	.67	.54	.54
Outing flannel night clothes	1	.71	.71	.57	.57	.75	.75	.85	.85	.62	.62
Cotton drawers	2	.38	.76	.32	.64	.39	.78	.44	.88	.45	.90
Wool drawers	2	.68	1.36	.80	1.60	.86	1.72	.86	1.72	.84	1.68
Underwaist	2	.35	.70	.35	.70	.38	.76	.32	.64	.43	.86
Cotton stockings	5	.28	1.40	.23	1.15	.25	1.25	.24	1.20	.25	1.25
Cotton socks	3	.26	.78	.26	.78	.28	.84	.28	.84	.24	.72
Sandals	1	1.09	1.09	1.02	1.02	1.09	1.09	1.08	1.08	.98	.98
High shoes	2	1.96	3.92	1.74	3.48	2.24	4.48	1.87	3.74	1.50	3.00
Rubbers	1	.82	.82	.75	.75	.78	.78	.81	.81	.83	.83
Wool mittens	1	.43	.43	.33	.33	.40	.40	.40	.40	.45	.45
Winter cap	1	.76	.76	.75	.75	.86	.86	1.04	1.04	.85	.85
Summer hat	1	.66	.66	.61	.61	.80	.80	.93	.93	.75	.75
Garters	2	.20	.40	.19	.38	.23	.46	.21	.42	.20	.40
Half-soles and heels	2	1.30	2.60	1.35	2.70	1.11	2.22	1.15	2.30	1.00	2.00
Incidentals			.50		.50		.50		.50		.50
Total			$27.13		$24.34		$27.74		$28.04		$25.16

social needs of the family were confined to church, movies, lodge, shopping, occasional trips and visits, that the more formal clothing of both man and wife were spared hard service by the custom of wearing special clothing while at work, thus reducing wear and tear on street costumes. The replacement of children's clothing was based on the length of the time given garments would probably fit as well as on the probable length of their wear.

The average minimum cost of clothing for one year for a man, for a woman and for children of three different ages, at prices prevailing in the spring of 1926, is given in Table 10. These costs were obtained by multiplying the quantity of each article supposed to be used each year by its average price. The amounts given assume that some items were made at home while others were bought ready to wear. The substitution of more home sewing might reduce the cost by insuring a better quality and, therefore, longer wear for the garments thus made, while purchasing everything ready made would probably increase the cost. Purchase of garments at sale prices or second hand would reduce the cost shown, while purchase on the installment plan would necessitate a larger outlay.

TABLE 11: AVERAGE MINIMUM COST OF CLOTHING FOR ONE YEAR FOR THE FAMILY OF AN INDUSTRIAL WORKER LIVING AT A FAIR AMERICAN STANDARD IN NEW YORK CITY, 1926

(National Industrial Conference Board)

Family of Man, Wife and—	Bronx	Brooklyn	Manhattan	Queens	Richmond
One child	$177.10	$163.25	$178.86	$170.61	$158.63
Two children	217.65	198.51	217.94	209.61	194.41
Three children	258.20	233.76	257.02	248.62	230.19

The combination of these individual clothing costs into minimum allowances for families with varying numbers of children is shown in Table 11. The average cost of clothing for one child was found by taking the arithmetic average of the cost for three, as itemized in Table 10. As already noted, the average price of one article may appear slightly high, of another, slightly low, because of the method of their collection. The total cost undoubtedly represents a fair average

TABLE 12: AVERAGE MINIMUM COST OF SUNDRIES FOR THE FAMILY OF AN INDUSTRIAL WORKER LIVING AT A FAIR AMERICAN STANDARD IN NEW YORK CITY, 1926

(National Industrial Conference Board)

Item for —	Bronx	Brooklyn	Manhattan	Queens	Richmond
Weekly Cost (itemized)					
Man, Wife, One Child					
Transportation					
To work	$0.60	$0.60	$0.60	$0.90	$0.96
For shopping, school, recreation, etc.	.30	.30	.30	.45	.54
Recreation	.55	.55	.55	.55	.55
Reading material, stationery, postage, telephone, etc.	.35	.35	.35	.35	.35
Medical care and sick benefits	.60	.60	.60	.60	.60
Insurance	.60	.60	.60	.60	.60
Organizations	.27	.27	.27	.27	.27
Church, charity, gifts	.50	.50	.50	.50	.50
Candy, tobacco, etc.	.50	.50	.50	.50	.50
Cleaning supplies and toilet requisites	.80	.80	.80	.80	.80
Furniture and furnishings	.55	.55	.55	.55	.55
Total	$5.62	$5.62	$5.62	$6.07	$6.22
Man, Wife, Two Children					
Transportation					
To work	$0.60	$0.60	$0.60	$0.90	$0.96
For shopping, school, recreation, etc.	.40	.40	.40	.60	.72
Recreation	.70	.70	.70	.70	.70
Reading material, stationery, postage, telephone, etc.	.35	.35	.35	.35	.35
Medical care and sick benefits	.80	.80	.80	.80	.80
Insurance	.70	.70	.70	.70	.70
Organizations	.29	.29	.29	.29	.29
Church, charity, gifts	.55	.55	.55	.55	.55
Candy, tobacco, etc.	.55	.55	.55	.55	.55
Cleaning supplies and toilet requisites	.90	.90	.90	.90	.90
Furniture and furnishings	.75	.75	.75	.75	.75
Total	$6.59	$6.59	$6.59	$7.09	$7.27

minimum allowance for clothing for individuals and families of the types specified, at 1926 prices.

SUNDRIES

Table 12 summarizes the estimated minimum cost of sundries for one week and for one year for families of different sizes in the separate boroughs of New York City, at

TABLE 12: AVERAGE MINIMUM COST OF SUNDRIES FOR THE FAMILY OF AN INDUSTRIAL WORKER LIVING AT A FAIR AMERICAN STANDARD IN NEW YORK CITY, 1926 (*Continued*)

(National Industrial Conference Board)

Item for —	Bronx	Brooklyn	Manhattan	Queens	Richmond
Man, Wife, Three Children					
Transportation					
To work	$0.60	$0.60	$0.60	$0.90	$0.96
For shopping, school, recreation, etc.	.50	.50	.50	.75	.90
Recreation	.85	.85	.85	.85	.85
Reading material, stationery, postage, telephone, etc.	.35	.35	.35	.35	.35
Medical care and sick benefits	1.00	1.00	1.00	1.00	1.00
Insurance	.80	.80	.80	.80	.80
Organizations	.31	.31	.31	.31	.31
Church, charity, gifts	.60	.60	.60	.60	.60
Candy, tobacco, etc.	.60	.60	.60	.60	.60
Cleaning supplies and toilet requisites	1.00	1.00	1.00	1.00	1.00
Furniture and furnishings	.75	.75	.75	.75	.75
Total	$7.36	$7.36	$7.36	$7.91	$8.12

Yearly Cost (total)

	Bronx	Brooklyn	Manhattan	Queens	Richmond
Man, Wife, One Child	$292.24	$292.24	$292.24	$315.64	$323.44
Man, Wife, Two Children	342.68	342.68	342.68	368.68	378.04
Man, Wife, Three Children	382.72	382.72	382.72	411.32	422.24

prices being asked in the spring of 1926. These estimates were based on the data given in Chapter V and need no further explanation here. The average cost of sundries for each child was determined from the average needs of an 8-year-old.

THE COMPLETE BUDGET

The relative cost of living from time to time or from place to place is dependent on a comparison of all the elements which go to make up the total cost of living. It is fairly customary, however, to judge these circumstances by the one or the few outstanding factors, give the others minor consideration or leave them out of account entirely. At the present moment, the item outstanding in the minds of most people is rent. This is particularly true if families are obliged for one reason or another to move. As pointed out several times in the present report, the rents which tenants pay in moving from one house to another are quite uniformly higher than those which as old tenants they have been paying for practically identical accommodations. This gives the impression that rents are rising, or that rents are higher in one section of the city than in another, whereas as a matter of fact the family moving into the place vacated by the first tenant will undoubtedly pay more as a new tenant than the old tenant paid.

Food may cost more in one section of the city than in another, depending on many circumstances, and this is especially true of articles in which there is a quality or demand element; gas or electricity rates may be higher or lower, also transportation costs and the like. These items stand out in the mind of the average consumer. But, no matter how important any one item or any group of items may be, there are sure to be many others making up the total cost of living. It is necessary, therefore, in determining what it really costs to live, to take a complete budget, worked out on a logically balanced basis.

From the present survey, it appears that when all the different factors are taken into account, there is a marked similarity in the cost of maintaining approximately the same standard of living in the different boroughs of New York City. For the family of an industrial worker, the difference between Brooklyn where the cost was the lowest, and Manhattan, the highest, was in the neighborhood of 3%. These figures, of course, measure material satisfactions. They afford little opportunity for comparison of what is obtained for the necessary outlay and doubtless these factors as well as habits to a large extent determine in what section of the city industrial families will live. From the point of view of minimum financial outlay there is little to choose.

A summary of the average minimum cost of all the goods and services required for the maintenance of a fair American standard of living by families of industrial workers in New York City at prices prevailing in the spring of 1926, itemized in the preceding pages, is given in Table 13. The estimates are made on the assumption that all of the housework, laundry, cooking and some of the sewing is done by the mother of the family; that there are no emergencies. There is nothing for a vacation, for unemployment, for old age, for

TABLE 13: AVERAGE MINIMUM COST OF MAINTAINING A FAIR AMERICAN STANDARD OF LIVING FOR THE FAMILY OF AN INDUSTRIAL WORKER IN NEW YORK CITY, 1926

(National Industrial Conference Board)

Family of Man, Wife and—	Bronx	Brooklyn	Manhattan	Queens	Richmond
			Yearly Cost[a]		
One child					
Housing	$306.00	$270.00	$306.00	$288.00	$252.00
Fuel and light	89.08	90.28	89.08	81.10	84.10
Food	528.84	533.00	529.36	529.36	549.64
Clothing	177.10	163.25	178.86	170.61	158.63
Sundries	292.24	292.24	292.24	315.64	323.44
Total	$1,393.26	$1,348.77	$1,395.54	$1,384.71	$1,367.81
Two children					
Housing	$408.00	$360.00	$408.00	$384.00	$336.00
Fuel and light	97.70	97.70	97.70	87.50	90.50
Food	645.32	650.52	645.84	645.84	670.28
Clothing	217.65	198.51	217.94	209.61	194.41
Sundries	342.68	342.68	342.68	368.68	378.04
Total	$1,711.35	$1,649.41	$1,712.16	$1,695.63	$1,669.23
Three children					
Housing	$408.00	$360.00	$408.00	$384.00	$336.00
Fuel and light	97.70	97.70	97.70	87.50	90.50
Food	761.80	767.52	762.32	762.32	791.44
Clothing	258.20	233.76	257.02	248.62	230.19
Sundries	382.72	382.72	382.72	411.32	422.24
Total	$1,908.42	$1,841.70	$1,907.76	$1,893.76	$1,870.37
			Weekly Cost[a]		
One child					
Housing	$5.88	$5.19	$5.88	$5.54	$4.85
Fuel and light	1.71	1.74	1.71	1.56	1.62
Food	10.17	10.25	10.18	10.18	10.57
Clothing	3.41	3.14	3.44	3.28	3.05
Sundries	5.62	5.62	5.62	6.07	6.22
Total	$26.79	$25.94	$26.83	$26.63	$26.31
Two children					
Housing	$7.85	$6.92	$7.85	$7.38	$6.46
Fuel and light	1.88	1.88	1.88	1.68	1.74
Food	12.41	12.51	12.42	12.42	12.89
Clothing	4.19	3.82	4.19	4.03	3.74
Sundries	6.59	6.59	6.59	7.09	7.27
Total	$32.92	$31.72	$32.93	$32.60	$32.10
Three children					
Housing	$7.85	$6.92	$7.85	$7.38	$6.46
Fuel and light	1.88	1.88	1.88	1.68	1.74
Food	14.65	14.76	14.66	14.66	15.22
Clothing	4.96	4.50	4.94	4.78	4.43
Sundries	7.36	7.36	7.36	7.91	8.12
Total	$36.70	$35.42	$36.69	$36.41	$35.97

[a] The weekly cost of housing, fuel and light and clothing was derived from the yearly cost. For the other items, the yearly cost was derived from the weekly. There is, therefore, a very slight discrepancy between the yearly and the weekly totals.

savings of any kind. On the other hand, bargain prices on clothing and furnishings, readjustments of certain items within the budget as it is allowed here, management superior to that assumed here, might reduce the necessary outlay a little.[1]

[1] Some estimates of the cost of living have reduced the final figures based on an itemized budget 5% or 10% to take account of possible savings through good management. See, for example, United States Bureau of Labor Statistics, "Tentative Quantity and Cost Budget," *op. cit.*, p. 10; Report of the California Cost of Living Survey, *op. cit.*, pp. 17; 20.

CHAPTER VII

COST OF LIVING FOR SINGLE PERSONS

YOUNG unmarried workers in New York City have several different varieties of living accommodations available. Among the youngest and, therefore, presumably the minimum standard industrial workers, it is customary for the boys and girls to live at home, either paying a fixed amount into the family treasury each week or paying in everything and receiving a fixed allowance back. The various organizations in the city which provide housing for men and women living apart from a family group report that almost none of their clients are the boys and girls of the minimum standard industrial worker class. The latter, if they do not live with their own families, so often live with friends or relatives as to create no special problem. Men alone in the city are sufficiently numerous, however, to demand some consideration as to their minimum cost of living. The estimate which has been made for a girl living at home as part of a family group may easily be readjusted, with the data given throughout this report, to cover the minimum needs of the boy who lives at home, also, if that is required, and from the data regarding the cost of paying commercial rates for room and board for a man, a fair estimate of similar expenses for a young woman living apart from a family group may be made. The costs in all instances are based on quotations secured in the spring of 1926.

SINGLE MALE WORKER

Young male industrial workers living apart from a family group usually rent a room with one or more other persons in like circumstances and get their meals in cafeterias and cheap restaurants. Their amusements are the movies and pool rooms as well as those that are afforded by the usual social activities of their class.

Lodging

The various organizations consulted, whose principal activities are with young men, estimated that furnished rooms suitable for young industrial workers cost from $3 a week up. If two or more shared a room in a lodging house, the cost would be considerably less than the outlay necessary for the rent of a single room with a private family. So far as could be ascertained the range of rents was about the same from borough to borough, but the accommodations to be secured undoubtedly differed greatly. Three dollars and a half a week was enough to allow as the minimum rent of a furnished room for a single male industrial worker in the spring of 1926 in Brooklyn, Queens and Richmond and $4 in Manhattan and the Bronx.

Food

Food was estimated by several authorities to require at least $1.25 a day outlay for young men eating in cafeterias and cheap restaurants. Combining the prices charged at a number of these into fairly balanced and substantial rations indicates that this amount was sufficient as a minimum in all boroughs.

Clothing

A single man may be expected to spend somewhat more for his clothing than a married man, not so much because of intrinsic needs for more or costlier garments as because what he has wears out more quickly if not kept in repair. Not having a wife to attend to these needs for him he must pay for this service or increase the replacement because of shortened durability. How much greater this cost of clothing is for a single man than for a married man would be difficult to estimate exactly, based as it is on so many variables. It has been assumed to add from 25% to 40%[1] to the cost of clothing as estimated for a married man. For purposes of the present study, 30% has been added to the cost of a married male industrial worker's clothing to determine the

[1] Special Report, No. 21, *op. cit.*, pp. 14, 31; William E. Mosher, "Quantity and Cost Budgets for Clerical Workers in New York City, April, 1921," issued by the Bureau of Municipal Research, New York, 1921, pp. 10, 21.

amount a single man should have for the same purpose each year, based on prices in the spring of 1926.

Sundries

A single man also spends more for sundries than a married man spends. His recreation must be sought outside his lodgings, which often do not afford a suitable place for meeting his friends; this means expenditure for entertainment for himself and also sometimes for others; his laundry must be paid for; if he becomes ill he may have to pay for attention which in the home would come free; he usually carries heavier insurance than a married man, as a means of saving. The estimated cost of sundries in the spring of 1926, on the basis of data already given in the preceding chapters, is shown in Table 14.

The Complete Budget

Table 14 also summarizes the minimum cost of maintaining a fair average American standard of living for single male industrial workers in New York City in the spring of 1926. These figures cover the obvious necessities of well-balanced living. Except for insurance, which in the case of the single man provides for somewhat more than mere burial expenses, there is no allowance for savings and nothing for a vacation. The single man has little opportunity, through good management, buying below the market rate and the like, to reduce his cost of living to less than the sums allowed. To the extent, however, that he is able to get a room for less than the amounts specified, that he does not have to pay so much carfare, that he may possibly be able to save on laundry and get his clothing at bargain prices, or that he may fortunately escape illness, he may be able to do better on the other items. Vice versa, of course, he may have to forego recreation, gifts and other sundry outlays to meet extraordinary expenses not provided for in the averages given here.

The figures in Table 14 show for a single male industrial worker, as other figures have shown for families in the separate boroughs, that there was very little difference in the cost of living as between different sections of New York City in the spring of 1926. Some items might be relatively high

TABLE 14: AVERAGE MINIMUM COST OF MAINTAINING A FAIR AMERICAN STANDARD OF LIVING FOR A SINGLE MALE INDUSTRIAL WORKER LIVING APART FROM A FAMILY GROUP IN NEW YORK CITY, 1926

(National Industrial Conference Board)

Item	Yearly Cost [a]					Weekly Cost [a]				
	Bronx	Brooklyn	Manhattan	Queens	Richmond	Bronx	Brooklyn	Manhattan	Queens	Richmond
Lodging	$208.00	$182.00	$208.00	$182.00	$182.00	$4.00	$3.50	$4.00	$3.50	$3.50
Food	455.00	455.00	455.00	455.00	455.00	8.75	8.75	8.75	8.75	8.75
Clothing	99.45	98.00	99.71	96.69	87.70	1.91	1.88	1.92	1.86	1.69
Sundries										
Transportation	41.60	41.60	41.60	62.40	68.64	.80	.80	.80	1.20	1.32
Recreation	20.80	20.80	20.80	20.80	20.80	.40	.40	.40	.40	.40
Reading material, stationery, postage, telephone, etc.	13.00	13.00	13.00	13.00	13.00	.25	.25	.25	.25	.25
Medical care and sick benefits	20.80	20.80	20.80	20.80	20.80	.40	.40	.40	.40	.40
Insurance	26.00	26.00	26.00	26.00	26.00	.50	.50	.50	.50	.50
Organizations	13.00	13.00	13.00	13.00	13.00	.25	.25	.25	.25	.25
Church, charity, gifts	10.40	10.40	10.40	10.40	10.40	.20	.20	.20	.20	.20
Tobacco, candy, etc.	15.60	15.60	15.60	15.60	15.60	.30	.30	.30	.30	.30
Toilet articles, haircuts, etc.	13.00	13.00	13.00	13.00	13.00	.25	.25	.25	.25	.25
Laundry	46.80	46.80	46.80	46.80	46.80	.90	.90	.90	.90	.90
Total	$983.45	$956.00	$983.71	$975.49	$972.74	$18.91	$18.38	$18.92	$18.76	$18.71

[a] The weekly cost of clothing was derived from the yearly; for all other items, the yearly cost was derived from the weekly. There is, therefore, a very slight discrepancy between the yearly and the weekly totals.

in one place, others in another, but the balanced level of all combined was about the same.

Single Female Worker

The United States Census of 1920 indicated that there were at that time nearly 700,000 females gainfully occupied in New York City. Of these, 313,120 were 15 years of age and under 25.[1] The great majority of these young women lived at home as a part of a family group. Not more than 20%, apparently, were without a permanent home in the city; indeed, this estimate is probably over liberal for the city as a whole.[2] Among those employed in the city's factories it is rare to find a young woman living apart from a family group; and among the younger employees in stores, offices, banks and similar occupations it is customary for them to live at home, turning their income over to the mother of the family each pay day and receiving back from her whatever is thought proper in the prevailing family circumstances. Sometimes the mother of the family purchases all of the girl's clothing for her, does her laundry and gives the girl only enough to pay for carfare, lunch and recreation; sometimes the girl has a fixed allowance, from which she pays for her clothing as well as incidental expenses.

Whether, in fact, what she actually turns in provides for her complete support, more or less, is no part of the present study. But since the majority of young female industrial workers in New York City live at home as part of a family group the minimum cost of living for such a young person is estimated on the basis of the cost of her fair share of family expenses. No estimate has been made of her cost of living if she was obliged to pay commercial rates for board and lodging. Instances where these are paid by minimum standard female industrial workers are relatively so rare as

[1] Fourteenth Census of the United States, Vol. IV, pp. 454–455.

[2] The Association to Promote Proper Housing for Girls estimates, for example, that about 20% of the gainfully employed females between the ages of 15 and 25 years in Manhattan were without a permanent home. This is probably high for the other boroughs, for while the proportion of all females gainfully employed in Manhattan is nearly 20% greater than the average for the city as a whole and among those between 15 and 25 the proportion averages about the same, Manhattan is the great employment center and the place to which persons of both sexes and all ages drift when they come to New York to seek their fortune.

not to require consideration in the present investigation, and, as already noted, such costs may be estimated, if required, from data given elsewhere in this report.

Home Expenses

The method of estimating a young girl's fair share of the living expenses of the family group of which she is a part, used in an earlier survey by the Board,[1] has been adopted for the present purpose. This was to assume that the young girl at home should bear the cost of one room in the apartment where she lives, since, although she may share her sleeping quarters, she may be expected to use the living room as much or more than other members of the family. Her fair share of heat and light may be apportioned on the same basis, namely, one-fourth the sum required to heat and light a four-room apartment. For food, the pro rata cost of her share may readily be obtained on the basis of energy values, as shown in Table 4.

In addition to shelter and food, however, the girl living at home is expected to pay her share of certain other joint expenses. Upkeep of furniture and furnishings, cooking, cleaning, laundry, sewing, shopping and numerous other services performed by the mother of the family are all legitimate if intangible costs.[2] The girl's share of household upkeep, like her share of housing and fuel and light costs, may be placed at one-quarter of the total family allowance for this item in a group with one or two younger children. If it be assumed that the mother of the family devotes approximately one-third of her efforts to the care of her grown daughter and two-thirds to her husband and dependent children, the cost of her own upkeep may be assumed to be borne in that proportion by the wage-earning members of the family. The grown daughter's share of payment for depreciation of household equipment and for services of the mother in the home is equal to approximately one-half of the home expenses which have a more tangible basis. Fifty per cent of the latter was, therefore, added to cover the maintenance

[1] Special Report No. 17, *op. cit.*, pp. 12–15.

[2] The daughter of the family often performs many of these services for herself and assists her mother in rendering service to other members of the family also.

TABLE 15: AVERAGE MINIMUM COST OF CLOTHING FOR ONE YEAR FOR A SINGLE FEMALE INDUSTRIAL WORKER LIVING AT A FAIR AMERICAN STANDARD IN NEW YORK CITY, 1926

(National Industrial Conference Board)

Item	Quantity Allowance	Bronx		Brooklyn		Manhattan		Queens		Richmond	
		Average Price	Yearly Cost	Average Price	Yearly Cost	Average Price	Yearly Cost	Average Price	Yearly Cost	Average Price	Yearly Cost
Coat	1	$13.06	$13.06	$10.50	$10.50	$14.90	$14.90	$13.67	$13.67	$11.25	$11.25
Sweater	½	3.15	1.58	2.30	1.15	3.30	1.65	3.68	1.84	2.32	1.16
Wool dress	1	10.01	10.01	5.83	5.83	6.29	6.29	8.12	8.12	7.50	7.50
Silk dress	1	9.98	9.98	7.14	7.14	8.32	8.32	8.84	8.84	9.61	9.61
Cotton dress	2	2.14	4.28	1.89	3.78	2.79	5.58	2.13	4.26	2.03	4.06
Apron	2	.31	.62	.33	.66	.51	1.02	.36	.72	.50	1.00
Cotton stockings	2	.31	.62	.32	.64	.28	.56	33	.66	.29	.58
Wool stockings	2	.80	1.60	.69	1.38	.86	1.72	.83	1.66	.76	1.52
Silk stockings	2	1.01	2.02	.83	1.66	1.04	2.08	.70	1.40	.87	1.74
Muslin nightgown	1	1.03	1.03	.81	.81	1.05	1.05	.91	.91	.90	.90
Outing flannel nightgown	1	1.06	1.06	.88	.88	1.03	1.03	.97	.97	.99	.99
Corset	1	1.23	1.23	1.11	1.11	1.80	1.80	1.22	1.22	1.15	1.15
Brassiere	2	.46	.92	.44	.88	.58	1.16	.45	.90	.46	.92
Cotton vest	2	.32	.64	.31	.62	.31	.62	.27	.54	.29	.58
Cotton bloomers	3	.61	1.83	.54	1.62	.54	1.62	.55	1.65	.54	1.62
Winter union suit	2	1.10	2.20	.85	1.70	1.19	2.38	1.09	2.18	1.18	2.36
Sateen dress slip	1	1.04	1.04	1.11	1.11	1.32	1.32	1.02	1.02	1.04	1.04
Cotton crepe kimono	¼	1.04	.26	1.46	.37	1.61	.40	1.71	.43	1.72	.43
Summer hat	1	3.77	3.77	1.91	1.91	2.96	2.96	2.31	2.31	2.74	2.74
Winter hat	1	2.73	2.73	1.91	1.91	2.91	2.91	2.31	2.31	2.74	2.74
Chamoisette gloves	1	.86	.86	.63	.63	.79	.79	.79	.79	.84	.84
Felt house slippers	⅓	.78	.26	.74	.25	.77	.26	.77	.26	.82	.27
Oxfords	1	4.22	4.22	3.98	3.98	4.75	4.75	4.04	4.04	3.26	3.26
Pumps	1	4.19	4.19	3.98	3.98	4.67	4.67	4.10	4.10	3.26	3.26
Rubbers	1	1.14	1.14	1.07	1.07	1.05	1.05	1.05	1.05	.96	.96
Umbrella	½	1.00	.50	.98	.49	1.25	.63	1.09	.55	1.25	.63
Handkerchief	8	.08	.64	.06	.48	.10	.80	.08	.64	.10	.80
Handbag	1	1.56	1.56	.80	.80	1.50	1.50	.90	.90	1.00	1.00
Cleaning and pressing	2	1.70	3.40	2.17	4.34	1.63	3.26	1.92	3.84	2.00	4.00
Half-soles and heels	2	1.44	2.88	1.25	2.50	1.31	2.62	1.25	2.50	1.50	3.00
Heels	2	.46	.92	.50	1.00	.44	.88	.50	1.00	.50	1.00
Incidentals			5.00		5.00		5.00		5.00		5.00
Total			$86.05		$70.18		$85.58		$80.28		$77.91

of household equipment and for the mother's services. The combination of this with the girl's fair share of the rent and the cost of fuel, light and food used by the family represents the contribution she must make to the household to cover the cost of her complete support while living at home, no more and no less.

Clothing

A young woman who goes to work every day requires more clothing, of a somewhat different kind from that of a woman in the home, whose outside activities are confined to marketing, taking the children out, going to church and having a limited number of excursions and other social engagements. The girl who travels back and forth to work on the subway, who must be out in all weathers, has a wear and tear on her clothing far greater than that of a woman whose traveling and other activities can be more readily adjusted to her convenience. Even though she changes her dress to uniform, apron or even old garments in the place of her employment, the girl in industry must look nicely on the street. Moreover, young girls, even with very limited incomes, have social demands not experienced by older married women, and for which they must be properly clothed. The allowances given in Table 15 are minimum, but with proper care they will suffice. If the young girl at work should elect to make some of her own dresses, a fairly common practice in these days of extreme simplicity in clothes, the cost would be materially reduced, or in other words, more would be available for the same outlay.

Sundries

The expenditures for sundries by a young wage earning woman would also be greater than those of a married woman of similar social position. On the basis of data given in Chapter V the estimated minimum outlay required for various sundries, in the spring of 1926, by a single female industrial worker living at a fair American standard, was as shown in Table 16.

8

Table 16: Average Minimum Cost of Maintaining a Fair American Standard of Living for a Single Female Industrial Worker Living as Part of a Family Group in New York City, 1926

(National Industrial Conference Board)

Item	Yearly Cost[a]					Weekly Cost[a]				
	Bronx	Brooklyn	Manhattan	Queens	Richmond	Bronx	Brooklyn	Manhattan	Queens	Richmond
Home expenses										
Lodging	$102.00	$90.00	$102.00	$96.00	$84.00	$1.96	$1.73	$1.96	$1.85	$1.62
Fuel and light	24.43	24.43	24.43	21.88	22.63	.47	.47	.47	.42	.44
Food	175.76	177.32	176.28	176.28	182.52	3.38	3.41	3.39	3.39	3.51
Upkeep, mother's services, etc.	151.10	145.88	151.36	147.08	144.58	2.91	2.81	2.91	2.83	2.78
Total home expenses	$453.29	$437.63	$454.07	$441.24	$433.53	$8.72	$8.42	$8.73	$8.49	$8.35
Clothing	86.05	70.18	85.58	80.28	77.91	1.65	1.35	1.65	1.54	1.50
Sundries										
Transportation	36.40	36.40	36.40	54.60	59.28	.70	.70	.70	1.05	1.14
Recreation	10.40	10.40	10.40	10.40	10.40	.20	.20	.20	.20	.20
Reading material, stationery, postage, telephone, etc.	10.40	10.40	10.40	10.40	10.40	.20	.20	.20	.20	.20
Medical care and sick benefits	10.40	10.40	10.40	10.40	10.40	.20	.20	.20	.20	.20
Insurance	13.00	13.00	13.00	13.00	13.00	.25	.25	.25	.25	.25
Organizations	5.20	5.20	5.20	5.20	5.20	.10	.10	.10	.10	.10
Church, charity, gifts	10.40	10.40	10.40	10.40	10.40	.20	.20	.20	.20	.20
Candy, etc.	7.80	7.80	7.80	7.80	7.80	.15	.15	.15	.15	.15
Vacation	20.80	20.80	20.80	20.80	20.80	.40	.40	.40	.40	.40
Toilet articles and services	13.00	13.00	13.00	13.00	13.00	.25	.25	.25	.25	.25
Total	$677.14	$645.61	$677.45	$677.52	$672.32	$13.02	$12.42	$13.03	$13.03	$12.94

[a] The weekly cost of lodging, fuel and light, clothing, upkeep and mother's services was derived from the yearly cost. For the other items, the yearly cost was derived from the weekly. There is, therefore, a very slight discrepancy between the yearly and the weekly totals.

The Complete Budget

The minimum cost of maintaining a fair American standard of living for a single female industrial worker living as a part of a family group in New York City, at prices prevailing in the spring of 1926, outlined above, is itemized in Table 16. These figures verify estimates already given for other types of living expenses, that the cost was nearly the same in all sections of the city at the same standard of living, although the means by which the necessities were supplied might differ considerably.

PART III: THE COST OF LIVING OF OFFICE WORKERS

Chart 2: Average Minimum Cost per Week of Maintaining a Fair American Standard of Living for the Family of an Office Worker in New York City, 1926

Based on figures in Table 23 and Table 28

(National Industrial Conference Board)

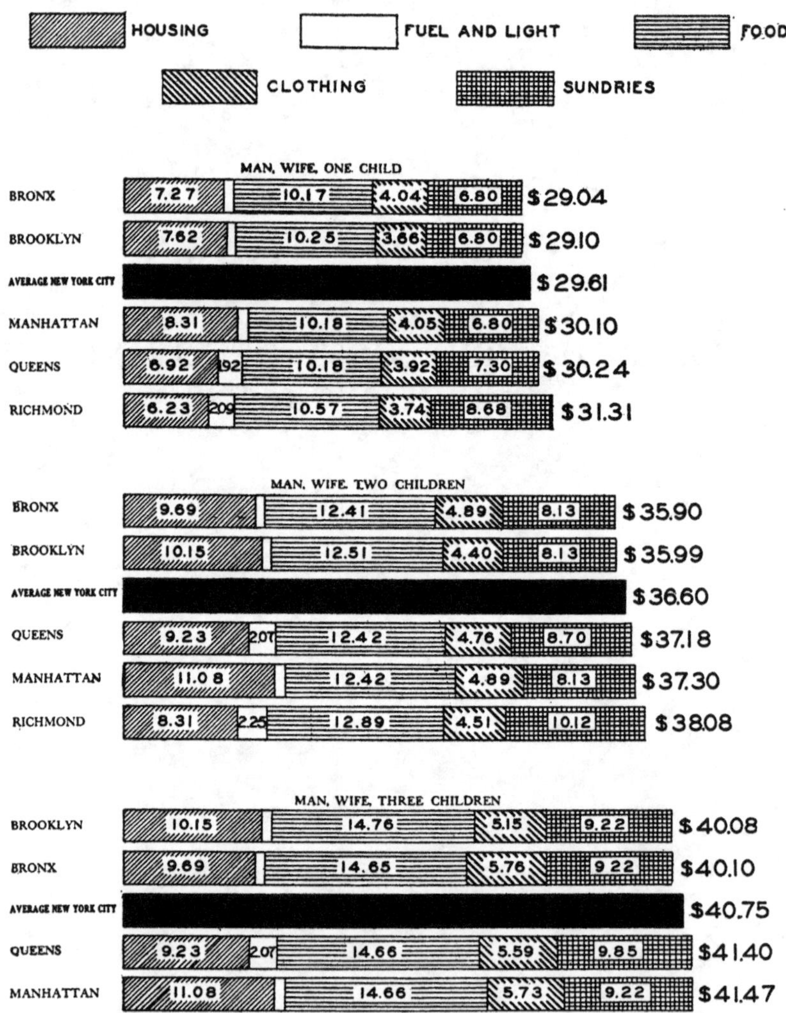

CHAPTER VIII

COST OF LIVING FOR FAMILIES

THE cost of living for an office worker's family differs in some respects from that of an industrial worker, not only because the nature of the man's employment dictates different food and clothing requirements, but also because certain undefined but none the less recognized social standards demand for their satisfaction varieties, qualities and quantities not required by the standards of the industrial worker's family.[1] With all of the data given in this report, however, there is no reason why any adjustments to meet the needs of either standard should not be made by those who for any reason require some other arrangement. The prices in all cases are averages of quotations collected in the spring of 1926; thus they are types rather than estimates of the cost of living of any particular family.

Housing

The housing of office workers in New York City varies. In the Bronx, Brooklyn and Manhattan, it is probably for the most part in the older steam heated apartments; in Queens and Richmond it is to be found in single or two family frame houses. The cost of housing presses heavily on families of this type and there is no reason to suppose that they do not get along with the least possible space. Three rooms, however, are minimum for such a family of three persons and four rooms are necessary for families with four or five members. The exact number of rooms specified may not be characteristic of the prevailing type of housing, since the older places almost invariably have more rather than fewer rooms than are allowed here as the minimum. It is assumed,

[1] It is true, of course, that the two are often combined, since it is fairly common in New York City for the children of industrial workers to enter office occupations. It has been assumed here that the occupation of the father sets the standard of living.

however, that the rent of the extra space will be covered by payment from an older child or other lodger. Hence, the man of the family may be assumed to be responsible only for such space as he and his dependent family occupy.

TABLE 17: AVERAGE MINIMUM OUTLAY NECESSARY FOR HOUSING FOR ONE MONTH AND FOR ONE YEAR FOR THE FAMILY OF AN OFFICE WORKER LIVING AT A FAIR AMERICAN STANDARD IN NEW YORK CITY, 1926[a]

(National Industrial Conference Board)

Family of Man, Wife and—	Bronx	Brooklyn	Manhattan	Queens	Richmond
			Monthly Cost		
(Average rent per room)....	\$10.50[b]	\$11.00[b]	\$12.00[b]	\$10.00[c]	\$9.00[c]
One child................	\$31.50	\$33.00	\$36.00	\$30.00	\$27.00
Two children............	42.00	44.00	48.00	40.00	36.00
Three children...........	42.00	44.00	48.00	40.00	36.00
			Yearly Cost		
One child................	\$378.00	\$396.00	\$432.00	\$360.00	\$324.00
Two children............	504.00	528.00	576.00	480.00	432.00
Three children...........	504.00	528.00	576.00	480.00	432.00

[a] These are for customary, not necessarily for identical, accommodations.
[b] Includes heat.
[c] Does not include heat.

The minimum cost of housing for an office worker's family as thus estimated is given in Table 17, based on rents in the spring of 1926. It should always be remembered that in no two places are the varieties of housing covered necessarily identical, but that each seems to be most characteristic of the housing of office workers in that particular locality. Nor can any comparison be made of the satisfactions to be secured from any two types of housing. If a family has resided all its life in the older boroughs, the old-fashioned and often inconvenient houses there are probably more precious than the newer buildings in the Bronx or Queens. The resident of Richmond or Queens, on the other hand, would find it a real hardship to give up his frame house, garden, space and sunshine, purchased though they may be at the expense of a tiresome journey to the place of his employment. All that the figures in Table 17 can show is the average outlay necessary for rent by the type of family specified, in the prevailing type of housing.

Fuel and Light

Inasmuch as the housing of families of office workers in New York City varies from one section to another, the allowance for fuel and light to supplement the cost of housing differs according to the services already included in the rent. In the steam heated apartments in the Bronx, Brooklyn and Manhattan, gas for cooking and electricity for lighting must be provided; in the more suburban areas of Queens and Richmond, coal for the furnace of a frame house must also be included. On this basis, Table 18 itemizes the minimum allowance necessary for fuel and light for an office worker's family living at a fair American standard in New York City in the spring of 1926. The figures in this table are based on the data given in Chapter II.

Table 18: Average Minimum Cost of Fuel and Light for One Year for the Family of an Office Worker Living at a Fair American Standard in New York City, 1926

(National Industrial Conference Board)

Family of Man, Wife and—	Bronx	Brooklyn	Manhattan	Queens	Richmond
One child[a]	$39.39[b]	$40.20[b]	$39.39[b]	$99.78[c]	$108.60[c]
Two children[d]	40.70[b]	41.60[b]	40.70[b]	107.80[e]	116.80[e]
Three children[d]	40.70[b]	41.60[b]	40.70[b]	107.80[e]	116.80[e]

[a] Three rooms.

[b] Steam-heated apartments; includes gas and electricity only.

[c] 10% less coal, kindling and electricity than in four rooms; 2,000 cubic feet gas per month.

[d] Four rooms.

[e] Four tons coal, $5 for kindling, 15 kwh. electricity and 2,000 cubic feet gas per month.

Food

The difference between the food requirements of sedentary workers and those at moderately active employment is about 10%, since adults engaged at less active labor require fewer energy units, and these of a less substantial kind, than do workers in heavier employments. Children need the same amount of energy, no matter what the occupation of their parents. The food costs, as estimated for the industrial worker's family, have, however, been adopted as representative of those of the office worker. Thus, by allowing the office worker's family to spend for food the same amount as the family of the industrial worker, although, in fact, fewer energy units are required, it is to be presumed that there will be more variety in the diet and that the food required will be secured from more expensive sources of energy than is permissible for the industrial worker's family on the same outlay. Celery and lettuce may be substituted for cabbage, for example; dry cereals for rolled oats; better cuts of beef may be purchased, or poultry used instead of lamb. Such changes would add delicacy and variety, but less nutriment would be purchased at the same cost as that allowed in the budget constructed for the family of the industrial worker.

A possible difference in the cost of food consumed by industrial and by office workers arises from the well-nigh universal custom among the latter of not taking their lunch from home but of buying it at a restaurant, cafeteria or lunch counter. This might add to the cost of food for an office worker's family. Assuming that the average cost of a week's allowance of food for a man living as a part of a family group is equivalent to his share of the total, based on calorie allowance, and that of his share, the cost of his breakfast and lunch together equal the cost of his dinner, then his lunch allowance is one-quarter of the total. The least money for which even a sandwich and glass of milk or cup of coffee can be obtained at a counter in the business sections of the different boroughs is 15 cents and frequently it is 20 cents. The difference between the cost of this for five days, and the allowance for the man's lunches in the family food budget must be added to the cost of his food. As a matter of fact, however, the man's share for lunch in the family budget as estimated on the basis of the needs of a man at moderately active labor so nearly approximates the cost of such food as is required for the lunch of a sedentary worker that no addition to the food budget seems necessary for this item.

Table 19, giving the average minimum food allowance for the family of an office worker living at a fair American standard in New York City in the spring of 1926, therefore, repeats the figures already given in Table 9 for an industrial worker's family.

TABLE 19: AVERAGE MINIMUM COST OF FOOD FOR ONE WEEK AND FOR ONE YEAR FOR THE FAMILY OF AN OFFICE WORKER LIVING AT A FAIR AMERICAN STANDARD IN NEW YORK CITY, 1926[a]

(National Industrial Conference Board)

Family of Man, Wife and—	Bronx	Brooklyn	Manhattan	Queens	Richmond
			Weekly Cost		
One child	$10.17	$10.25	$10.18	$10.18	$10.57
Two children	12.41	12.51	12.42	12.42	12.89
Three children	14.65	14.76	14.66	14.66	15.22
			Yearly Cost		
One child	$528.84	$533.00	$529.36	$529.36	$549.64
Two children	645.32	650.52	645.84	645.84	670.28
Three children	761.80	767.52	762.32	762.32	791.44

[a] Includes allowance for man's lunch to be eaten at a restaurant.

CLOTHING

The minimum clothing budgets constructed for an office worker and his family recognize the fact that the man at a desk job cannot wear a khaki shirt and overalls and that not only the kind of clothing but also the length of time it can be worn is somewhat different for an office worker than for an industrial worker. For his family, also, there are certain intangible differences in clothing requirements, based on somewhat wider social contacts and more or less well-established standards. There is, therefore, a redistribution of quantities allowed although the qualities are the same in both budgets.

The average cost of clothing for a year for an office worker, for the wife of an office worker and for his children of three different ages is given in Table 20. These costs were obtained by multiplying the quantity of each article required for a year's use by its average minimum price in the spring of 1926. Costs in all cases refer to articles purchased ready to wear. If some of the garments for the woman and children were to be made at home, the cost would be reduced, because of better quality and longer durability, or, for the amount specified, more articles might be obtained. Furthermore, if the woman of the family were in a position to take advantage of sales or could buy certain items out of season, substantial

TABLE 20A: AVERAGE MINIMUM COST OF CLOTHING FOR ONE YEAR FOR A MARRIED MALE OFFICE WORKER LIVING AT A FAIR AMERICAN STANDARD IN NEW YORK CITY, 1926

(National Industrial Conference Board)

Item	Quantity Allowance	Bronx		Brooklyn		Manhattan		Queens		Richmond	
		Average Price	Yearly Cost	Average Price	Yearly Cost	Average Price	Yearly Cost	Average Price	Yearly Cost	Average Price	Yearly Cost
Suit	1	$19.91	$19.91	$19.62	$19.62	$19.73	$19.73	$20.40	$20.40	$16.45	$16.45
Overcoat	1/3	18.90	6.30	19.33	6.44	21.32	7.11	21.42	7.14	21.05	7.02
Extra trousers	1	3.42	3.42	3.88	3.88	3.86	3.86	3.14	3.14	3.37	3.37
Sweater	1/2	4.16	2.08	3.59	1.80	3.85	1.93	3.32	1.66	2.83	1.42
Madras shirt	5	1.41	7.05	1.47	7.35	1.54	7.70	1.47	7.35	1.45	7.25
Oxfords	1	4.76	4.76	4.73	4.73	4.84	4.84	4.58	4.58	3.77	3.77
High shoes	1	4.77	4.77	4.82	4.82	5.07	5.07	4.48	4.48	3.65	3.65
Rubbers	1/2	1.36	.68	1.35	.68	1.36	.68	1.32	.66	1.35	.68
Cotton socks	8	.23	1.84	.22	1.76	.22	1.76	.19	1.52	.21	1.68
Summer union suit	2	1.17	2.34	.99	1.98	1.03	2.06	.98	1.96	.92	1.84
Winter union suit	1	1.48	1.48	1.46	1.46	1.48	1.48	1.49	1.49	1.48	1.48
Night clothes	2	1.43	2.86	1.42	2.84	1.37	2.74	1.33	2.66	1.38	2.76
Felt hat	1	3.42	3.42	3.03	3.03	2.96	2.96	3.41	3.41	3.29	3.29
Straw hat	1	2.19	2.19	1.80	1.80	1.96	1.96	1.74	1.74	1.80	1.80
Wool gloves	1/2	.94	.47	.88	.44	.86	.43	.84	.42	.87	.44
Kid gloves	1/2	2.07	1.04	2.26	1.13	1.96	.98	2.10	1.05	2.14	1.07
Tie	3	.70	2.10	.62	1.86	.73	2.19	.58	1.74	.52	1.56
Collar	12	.20	2.40	.19	2.28	.19	2.28	.20	2.40	.21	2.52
Garters	2	.26	.52	.25	.50	.28	.56	.25	.50	.24	.48
Belt	1	.57	.57	.62	.62	.65	.65	.51	.51	.47	.47
White handkerchief	8	.10	.80	.09	.72	.10	.80	.09	.72	.10	.80
Umbrella	1/3	1.44	.48	1.19	.40	1.27	.42	1.05	.35	1.25	.42
Half-soles and heels	2	1.75	3.50	1.65	3.30	1.56	3.12	1.56	3.12	1.75	3.50
Cleaning and pressing suit	2	1.50	3.00	1.69	3.38	1.41	2.82	1.67	3.34	1.50	3.00
Pressing suit	2	.46	.92	.50	1.00	.45	.90	.50	1.00	.50	1.00
Incidentals			1.00		1.00		1.00		1.00		1.00
Total			$79.90		$78.82		$80.03		$78.34		$72.72

TABLE 20B: AVERAGE MINIMUM COST OF CLOTHING FOR ONE YEAR FOR THE WIFE OF AN OFFICE WORKER LIVING AT A FAIR AMERICAN STANDARD IN NEW YORK CITY, 1926
(National Industrial Conference Board)

Item	Quantity Allowance	Bronx		Brooklyn		Manhattan		Queens		Richmond	
		Average Price	Yearly Cost	Average Price	Yearly Cost	Average Price	Yearly Cost	Average Price	Yearly Cost	Average Price	Yearly Cost
Coat	½	$13.06	$6.53	$10.50	$5.25	$14.90	$7.45	$13.67	$6.84	$11.25	$5.63
Suit	½	14.83	7.42	16.21	8.11	15.35	7.68	18.57	9.29	19.75	9.88
Sweater	½	3.15	1.58	2.30	1.15	3.30	1.65	3.68	1.84	2.32	1.16
Wool dress	½	10.01	5.01	5.83	2.92	6.29	3.15	8.12	4.06	7.50	3.75
Silk dress	½	9.98	4.99	7.14	3.57	8.32	4.16	8.84	4.42	9.61	4.81
Cotton dress	2	2.14	4.28	1.89	3.78	2.79	5.58	2.13	4.26	2.03	4.06
House dress	2	.86	1.72	.75	1.50	1.07	2.14	.97	1.94	1.15	2.30
Silk overblouse	1	4.40	4.40	3.30	3.30	4.04	4.04	4.09	4.09	3.87	3.87
Cotton overblouse	1	.151	1.51	1.21	1.21	1.35	1.35	1.53	1.53	1.32	1.32
Apron	2	.31	.62	.33	.66	.51	1.02	.36	.72	.50	1.00
Cotton stockings	2	.31	.62	.32	.64	.28	.56	.33	.66	.29	.58
Wool stockings	2	.80	1.60	.69	1.38	.86	1.72	.83	1.66	.76	1.52
Silk stockings	2	1.01	2.02	.83	1.66	1.04	2.08	.70	1.40	.87	1.74
Muslin nightgown	1	1.03	1.03	.81	.81	1.05	1.05	.91	.91	.90	.90
Outing flannel nightgown	1	1.06	1.06	.88	.88	1.03	1.03	.97	.97	.99	.99
Corset	2	1.23	2.46	1.11	2.22	1.80	3.60	1.22	2.44	1.15	2.30
Brassiere	2	.46	.92	.44	.88	.58	1.16	.45	.90	.46	.92
Cotton vest	2	.32	.64	.31	.62	.31	.62	.27	.54	.29	.58
Cotton bloomers	3	.61	1.83	.54	1.62	.54	1.62	.55	1.65	.54	1.62
Winter union suit	2	1.10	2.20	.85	1.70	1.19	2.38	1.09	2.18	1.18	2.36
Sateen dress slip	1	1.04	1.04	1.11	1.11	1.32	1.32	1.02	1.02	1.04	1.04
Cotton crepe kimono	⅓	1.04	.35	1.46	.49	1.61	.54	1.71	.57	1.72	.57
Summer hat	1½	3.77	5.66	1.91	2.87	2.96	4.44	2.31	3.47	2.74	4.11
Winter hat	1	2.73	2.73	1.91	1.91	2.91	2.91	2.31	2.31	2.74	2.74
Chamoisette gloves	1½	.86	1.29	.63	.95	.79	1.19	.79	1.19	.84	1.26
Felt house slippers	⅓	.78	.26	.74	.25	.77	.26	.77	.26	.82	.27
Oxfords	1	4.22	4.22	3.98	3.98	4.75	4.75	4.04	4.04	3.26	3.26
Pumps	1	4.19	4.19	3.98	3.98	4.67	4.67	4.10	4.10	3.26	3.26
Rubbers	½	1.14	.57	1.07	.54	1.05	.53	1.05	.53	.96	.48
Umbrella	¼	1.00	.25	.98	.25	1.25	.31	1.09	.27	1.25	.31
Handkerchief	6	.08	.48	.06	.36	.10	.60	.08	.48	.10	.60
Handbag	½	1.56	.78	.80	.40	1.50	.75	.90	.45	1.00	.50
Cleaning and pressing	2	1.70	3.40	2.17	4.34	1.63	3.26	1.92	3.84	2.00	4.00
Half-soles and heels	1½	1.44	2.16	1.25	1.88	1.31	1.97	1.25	1.88	1.50	2.25
Heels	1	.46	.46	.50	.50	.44	.44	.50	.50	.50	.50
Incidentals			5.00		5.00		5.00		5.00		5.00
Total			$85.28		$72.67		$86.98		$82.21		$81.44

TABLE 20C: AVERAGE MINIMUM COST OF CLOTHING FOR ONE YEAR FOR THE 12-YEAR-OLD SON OF AN OFFICE WORKER LIVING AT A FAIR AMERICAN STANDARD IN NEW YORK CITY, 1926

(National Industrial Conference Board)

Item	Quantity Allowance	Bronx		Brooklyn		Manhattan		Queens		Richmond	
		Average Price	Yearly Cost	Average Price	Yearly Cost	Average Price	Yearly Cost	Average Price	Yearly Cost	Average Price	Yearly Cost
Mackinaw	½	$8.33	$4.17	$5.70	$2.85	$6.71	$3.36	$6.56	$3.28	$6.19	$3.10
Sweater	½	2.94	1.47	2.46	1.23	2.71	1.36	2.55	1.28	2.66	1.33
Two-trouser suit	1	9.61	9.61	7.57	7.57	9.02	9.02	8.93	8.93	8.04	8.04
Heavy cotton trousers	3	1.70	5.10	1.27	3.81	1.63	4.89	1.41	4.23	1.46	4.38
Shirt or blouse	5	.89	4.45	.54	2.70	.87	4.35	.75	3.75	.97	4.85
Winter union suit	2	1.15	2.30	.89	1.78	.93	1.86	.95	1.90	1.05	2.10
Summer union suit	2	.72	1.44	.52	1.04	.54	1.08	.54	1.08	.70	1.40
Night clothes	2	1.09	2.18	.92	1.84	1.09	2.18	1.06	2.12	.99	1.98
Wool stockings	2	.76	1.52	.66	1.32	.64	1.28	.72	1.44	.71	1.42
Cotton stockings	10	.28	2.80	.30	3.00	.31	3.10	.29	2.90	.29	2.90
Oxfords	1	3.22	3.22	3.07	3.07	3.21	3.21	3.26	3.26	2.59	2.59
Sneakers	1	1.16	1.16	1.12	1.12	1.33	1.33	1.40	1.40	1.10	1.10
High shoes	2	3.26	6.52	3.09	6.18	3.29	6.58	3.27	6.54	2.62	5.24
Rubbers	1	1.07	1.07	1.02	1.02	1.06	1.06	1.08	1.08	1.04	1.04
Wool gloves	1	.61	.61	.56	.56	.53	.53	.53	.53	.58	.58
Winter cap	1	.92	.92	.95	.95	.98	.98	1.08	1.08	.90	.90
Summer hat	1	1.05	1.05	.87	.87	.88	.88	1.03	1.03	.88	.88
Necktie	3	.42	1.26	.33	.99	.34	1.02	.38	1.14	.38	1.14
Handkerchief	8	.07	.56	.07	.56	.09	.72	.08	.64	.08	.64
Belt	½	.43	.22	.37	.19	.37	.19	.41	.21	.32	.16
Garters	2[a]	.08	.16	.13	.26	.11	.22	.12	.24	.10	.20
Half-soles and heels	3	1.30	3.90	1.35	4.05	1.11	3.33	1.15	3.45	1.00	3.00
Incidentals			.50		.50		.50		.50		.50
Total			$56.19		$47.46		$53.03		$52.01		$49.47

[a] Material from which garters are made.

TABLE 20D: AVERAGE MINIMUM COST OF CLOTHING FOR ONE YEAR FOR THE 8-YEAR-OLD DAUGHTER OF AN OFFICE WORKER LIVING AT A FAIR AMERICAN STANDARD IN NEW YORK CITY, 1926

(National Industrial Conference Board)

Item	Quantity Allowance	Bronx		Brooklyn		Manhattan		Queens		Richmond	
		Average Price	Yearly Cost	Average Price	Yearly Cost	Average Price	Yearly Cost	Average Price	Yearly Cost	Average Price	Yearly Cost
Coat	½	$6.64	$3.32	$5.22	$2.61	$6.53	$3.27	$6.73	$3.37	$6.03	$3.02
Sweater	½	2.66	1.33	2.27	1.14	2.40	1.20	2.72	1.36	2.56	1.28
Wool dress (with bloomers)	½	3.42	1.71	3.02	1.51	3.62	1.81	3.73	1.87	3.62	1.81
Cotton dress (with bloomers)	6	1.18	7.08	.96	5.76	1.46	8.76	1.32	7.92	1.32	7.92
Slip	1	.65	.65	.56	.56	.68	.68	.63	.63	.68	.68
Bloomers	6	.45	2.70	.53	3.18	.38	2.28	.39	2.34	.39	2.34
Winter union suit	2	1.10	2.20	.87	1.74	.91	1.82	1.00	2.00	.97	1.94
Summer union suit	2	.78	1.56	.51	1.02	.57	1.14	.58	1.16	.62	1.24
Night clothes	2	.67	1.34	.59	1.18	.69	1.38	.83	1.66	.61	1.22
Underwaist	3	.39	1.17	.37	1.11	.39	1.18	.34	1.02	.40	1.20
Wool stockings	2	.67	1.34	.59	1.18	.66	1.32	.66	1.32	.66	1.32
Cotton stockings	6	.32	1.92	.28	1.68	.28	1.68	.28	1.68	.28	1.68
Oxfords	1	3.20	3.20	2.58	2.58	3.04	3.04	3.05	3.05	2.28	2.28
Sneakers	1	1.10	1.10	1.09	1.09	1.18	1.18	1.28	1.28	1.09	1.09
High shoes	2	3.24	6.48	2.78	5.56	3.35	6.70	3.15	6.30	2.24	4.48
Rubbers	1	.93	.93	.88	.88	.89	.89	.98	.98	.95	.95
Wool gloves	1	.58	.58	.54	.54	.51	.51	.55	.55	.55	.55
Winter hat	1	1.93	1.93	1.45	1.45	1.69	1.69	1.48	1.48	1.48	1.48
Summer hat	1	1.75	1.75	1.47	1.47	1.70	1.70	1.63	1.63	1.48	1.48
Handkerchief	8	.08	.64	.06	.48	.10	.80	.08	.64	.10	.80
Garters	2[a]	.08	.16	.13	.26	.11	.22	.12	.24	.10	.20
Half-soles and heels	3	1.30	3.90	1.35	4.05	1.11	3.33	1.15	3.45	1.00	3.00
Incidentals			.50		.50		.50		.50		.50
Total			$47.49		$41.53		$47.07		$46.43		$42.46

[a] Material from which garters are made.

TABLE 20E: AVERAGE MINIMUM COST OF CLOTHING FOR ONE YEAR FOR THE 2-YEAR-OLD SON OF AN OFFICE WORKER LIVING AT A FAIR AMERICAN STANDARD IN NEW YORK CITY, 1926

(National Industrial Conference Board)

Item	Quantity Allowance	Bronx		Brooklyn		Manhattan		Queens		Richmond	
		Average Price	Yearly Cost	Average Price	Yearly Cost	Average Price	Yearly Cost	Average Price	Yearly Cost	Average Price	Yearly Cost
Knitted suit	½	$4.56	$2.28	$4.28	$2.14	$4.57	$2.29	$4.85	$2.43	$4.61	$2.31
Sweater	1	2.30	2.30	1.49	1.49	1.78	1.78	1.92	1.92	2.09	2.09
Rompers	4	.73	2.92	.61	2.44	.79	3.16	.86	3.44	.66	2.64
Overalls	2	.62	1.24	.50	1.00	.62	1.24	.61	1.22	.53	1.06
Summer undershirt	3	.22	.66	.22	.66	.27	.81	.35	1.05	.31	.93
Winter undershirt	2	.83	1.66	.59	1.18	.69	1.38	.76	1.52	.64	1.28
Muslin night clothes	1	.66	.66	.54	.54	.72	.72	.67	.67	.54	.54
Outing flannel night clothes	1	.71	.71	.57	.57	.75	.75	.85	.85	.62	.62
Cotton drawers	3	.38	1.14	.32	.96	.39	1.17	.44	1.32	.45	1.35
Wool drawers	2	.68	1.36	.80	1.60	.86	1.72	.86	1.72	.84	1.68
Underwaist	2	.35	.70	.35	.70	.38	.76	.32	.64	.43	.86
Cotton stockings	6	.28	1.68	.23	1.38	.25	1.50	.24	1.44	.25	1.50
Cotton socks	4	.26	1.04	.26	1.04	.28	1.12	.28	1.12	.24	.96
Sandals	2	1.09	2.18	1.02	2.04	1.09	2.18	1.08	2.16	.98	1.96
High shoes	2	1.96	3.92	1.74	3.48	2.24	4.48	1.87	3.74	1.50	3.00
Rubbers	1	.82	.82	.75	.75	.78	.78	.81	.81	.83	.83
Wool mittens	1	.43	.43	.33	.33	.40	.40	.40	.40	.45	.45
Winter cap	1	.76	.76	.75	.75	.86	.86	1.04	1.04	.85	.85
Summer hat	1	.66	.66	.61	.61	.80	.80	.93	.93	.75	.75
Garters	2	.20	.40	.19	.38	.23	.46	.21	.42	.20	.40
Half-soles and heels	2	1.30	2.60	1.35	2.70	1.11	2.22	1.15	2.30	1.00	2.00
Incidentals			.50		.50		.50		.50		.50
Total			$30.62		$27.24		$31.08		$31.64		$28.56

savings might be effected. Purchasing clothing on the installment plan would almost certainly add to the costs given here.

The average annual cost of clothing for the family of an office worker with one, two or three children, at prices prevailing in the spring of 1926, is given in Table 21. The average cost of clothing for one child was found by taking the arithmetic average of the cost for the three, as itemized in Table 20.

TABLE 21: AVERAGE MINIMUM COST OF CLOTHING FOR ONE YEAR FOR THE FAMILY OF AN OFFICE WORKER LIVING AT A FAIR AMERICAN STANDARD IN NEW YORK CITY, 1926

(National Industrial Conference Board)

Family of Man, Wife and—	Bronx	Brooklyn	Manhattan	Queens	Richmond
One child................	$209.95	$190.23	$210.74	$203.91	$194.32
Two children............	245.22	228.97	254.47	247.27	234.48
Three children	299.48	267.71	298.20	290.63	274.64

SUNDRIES

From the data given in Chapter V, Table 22 has been constructed, showing the estimated minimum cost of sundries for families of different sizes among office workers living at a fair American standard in New York City in the spring of 1926. The average cost of sundries which was added or subtracted for each child is based on the possible needs of an 8-year-old. The allowances for many items are arbitrary; others are the best estimates of average minimum requirements possible under the circumstances. If they do not meet the needs of any individual or group, they may easily be changed, since their basis in all cases has been given.

THE COMPLETE BUDGET

The minimum cost of living for the family of an office worker living at a fair American standard and based on a balanced consumption of all the goods and services making up the total cost of living, summarized in Table 23, shows a striking similarity in different sections of New York City in the spring of 1926. Except for Richmond, where the estimated carfare raised the cost above that of the other boroughs, there seemed little to choose from the point of view of necessary outlay, slightly more than a dollar a week being the average difference in cost between living in the Bronx or Brooklyn on the one hand, or Manhattan or Queens on the other.

The housing problem was found to be as difficult for the families of office workers in New York City as for any other group, if not more so, since apparently the demand for low priced housing in desirable neighborhoods has far outrun the supply. The family which wishes to continue living according to the standards of its class has a hard time finding a place within its means if for any reason moving is required. Of all the housing inspected in the present survey that for which the most persistent hunting seemed necessary was housing of the kind which would appeal to persons of some education and refinement but moderate means. Persons now occupying such premises hesitate to move unless absolutely forced to do so, for they know that going into another place as a new tenant will be almost certain to increase the outlay they must make for rent. Especially among persons

TABLE 22: AVERAGE MINIMUM COST OF SUNDRIES FOR THE FAMILY OF AN OFFICE WORKER LIVING AT A FAIR AMERICAN STANDARD IN NEW YORK CITY, 1926

(National Industrial Conference Board)

Item for—	Bronx	Brooklyn	Manhattan	Queens	Richmond
Weekly Cost (itemized)					
Man, wife, one child					
Transportation					
To work	$0.60	$0.60	$0.60	$0.90	$2.16[a]
For shopping, school, recreation, etc.	.40	.40	.40	.60	.72
Recreation	.55	.55	.55	.55	.55
Reading material, stationery, postage, telephone, etc.	.50	.50	.50	.50	.50
Medical care and sick benefits	.60	.60	.60	.60	.60
Insurance	.85	.85	.85	.85	.85
Organizations	.35	.35	.35	.35	.35
Church, charity, gifts	.50	.50	.50	.50	.50
Candy, tobacco, etc.	.50	.50	.50	.50	.50
Cleaning supplies and toilet requisites	1.30	1.30	1.30	1.30	1.30
Furniture and furnishings	.65	.65	.65	.65	.65
Total	$6.80	$6.80	$6.80	$7.30	$8.68

TABLE 22: AVERAGE MINIMUM COST OF SUNDRIES FOR THE FAMILY OF AN OFFICE WORKER LIVING AT A FAIR AMERICAN STANDARD IN NEW YORK CITY, 1926—(*Continued*)

(National Industrial Conference Board)

Item for—	Bronx	Brooklyn	Manhattan	Queens	Richmond
			Weekly Cost (itemized)		
Man, wife, two children					
Transportation					
To work	$0.60	$0.60	$0.60	$0.90	$2.16[a]
For shopping, school, recreation, etc.	.53	.53	.53	.80	.96
Recreation	.70	.70	.70	.70	.70
Reading material, stationery, postage, telephone, etc.	.50	.50	.50	.50	.50
Medical care and sick benefits	.80	.80	.80	.80	.80
Insurance	.95	.95	.95	.95	.95
Organizations	.40	.40	.40	.40	.40
Church, charity, gifts	.55	.55	.55	.55	.55
Candy, tobacco, etc.	.55	.55	.55	.55	.55
Cleaning supplies and toilet requisites	1.65	1.65	1.65	1.65	1.65
Furniture and furnishings	.90	.90	.90	.90	.90
Total	$8.13	$8.13	$8.13	$8.70	$10.12
Man, wife, three children					
Transportation					
To work	$0.60	$0.60	$0.60	$0.90	$2.16[a]
For shopping, school, recreation, etc.	.67	.67	.67	1.00	1.20
Recreation	.85	.85	.85	.85	.85
Reading material, stationery, postage, telephone, etc.	.50	.50	.50	.50	.50
Medical care and sick benefits	1.00	1.00	1.00	1.00	1.00
Insurance	1.05	1.05	1.05	1.05	1.05
Organizations	.45	.45	.45	.45	.45
Church, charity, gifts	.60	.60	.60	.60	.60
Candy, tobacco, etc.	.60	.60	.60	.60	.60
Cleaning supplies and toilet requisites	2.00	2.00	2.00	2.00	2.00
Furniture and furnishings	.90	.90	.90	.90	.90
Total	$9.22	$9.22	$9.22	$9.85	$11.31
			Yearly Cost (total)		
Man, wife, one child	$353.60	$353.60	$353.60	$379.60	$451.36
Man, wife, two children	422.76	422.76	422.76	452.40	526.24
Man, wife, three children	479.44	479.44	479.44	512.20	588.12

[a] To work in the other boroughs as well as in Richmond.

Table 23: Average Minimum Cost of Maintaining a Fair American Standard of Living for the Family of an Office Worker in New York City, 1926

(National Industrial Conference Board)

Family of Man, Wife and—	Bronx	Brooklyn	Manhattan	Queens	Richmond
			Yearly Cost[a]		
One child					
Housing	$378.00[b]	$396.00[b]	$432.00[b]	$360.00[c]	$324.00[c]
Fuel and light	39.39[d]	40.20[d]	39.39[d]	99.78[e]	108.60[e]
Food	528.84	533.00	529.36	529.36	549.64
Clothing	209.95	190.23	210.74	203.91	194.32
Sundries	353.60	353.60	353.60	379.60	451.36[f]
Total	$1,509.78	$1,513.03	$1,565.09	$1,572.65	$1,627.92[f]
Two children					
Housing	$504.00[b]	$528.00[b]	$576.00[b]	$480.00[c]	$432.00[c]
Fuel and light	40.70[d]	41.60[d]	40.70[d]	107.80[e]	116.80[e]
Food	645.32	650.52	645.84	645.84	670.28
Clothing	254.22	228.97	254.47	247.27	234.48
Sundries	422.76	422.76	422.76	452.40	526.24[f]
Total	$1,867.00	$1,871.85	$1,939.77	$1,933.31	$1,979.80[f]
Three children					
Housing	$504.00[b]	$528.00[b]	$576.00[b]	$480.00[c]	$432.00[c]
Fuel and light	40.70[d]	41.60[d]	40.70[d]	107.80[e]	116.80[e]
Food	761.80	767.52	762.32	762.32	791.44
Clothing	299.48	267.71	298.20	290.63	274.64
Sundries	479.44	479.44	479.44	512.20	588.12[f]
Total	$2,085.42	$2,084.27	$2,156.66	$2.152.95	$2,203.00[f]
			Weekly Cost[a]		
One child					
Housing	$7.27[b]	$7.62[b]	$8.31[b]	$6.92[c]	$6.23[c]
Fuel and light	.76[d]	.77[d]	.76[d]	1.92[e]	2.09[e]
Food	10.17	10.25	10.18	10.18	10.57
Clothing	4.04	3.66	4.05	3.92	3.74
Sundries	6.80	6.80	6.80	7.30	8.68[f]
Total	$29.04	$29.10	$30.10	$30.24	$31.31[f]
Two children					
Housing	$9.69[b]	$10.15[b]	$11.08[b]	$9.23[c]	$8.31[c]
Fuel and light	.78[d]	.80[d]	.78[d]	2.07[e]	2.25[e]
Food	12.41	12.51	12.42	12.42	12.89
Clothing	4.89	4.40	4.89	4.76	4.51
Sundries	8.13	8.13	8.13	8.70	10.12[f]
Total	$35.90	$35.99	$37.30	$37.18	$38.08[f]
Three children					
Housing	$9.69[b]	$10.15[b]	$11.08[b]	$9.23[c]	$8.31[c]
Fuel and light	.78[d]	.80[d]	.78[d]	2.07[e]	2.25[e]
Food	14.65	14.76	14.66	14.66	15.22
Clothing	5.76	5.15	5.73	5.59	5.28
Sundries	9.22	9.22	9.22	9.85	11.31[f]
Total	$40.10	$40.08	$41.47	$41.40	$42.37[f]

[a] The weekly cost of housing, fuel and light and clothing was derived from the yearly cost; for the other items, the yearly cost was derived from the weekly. There is, therefore, a very slight discrepancy between the yearly and the weekly to tals. [b] Includes heat. [c] Does not include heat.

[d] Gas and electricity only, for steam heated apartment.

[e] Coal, kindling, gas and electricity for frame house or floor in two family house.

[f] Includes transportation to work in other boroughs.

who have lived in the same place for many years and whose rent accordingly has been advanced relatively little above the pre-war level, there is real tragedy in the heartbreaking hunt for a new place in any way comparable with the old. The rents given here as the estimated minimum are those which a new tenant would be required to pay for a house or apartment; they are not the averages of rents being paid at the present time.

Another circumstance to remember in connection with the relative cost of housing is that some rents include heat while others do not. The places in which office workers were living in the Bronx, Brooklyn and Manhattan for the most part were heated apartments; in Queens and Richmond, on the other hand, single or two family frame dwellings almost exclusively provided shelter for this type of family. When the cost of heating, at the prevailing price of coal, is taken into account, the necessary outlay for rent, fuel and light combined is not so very different.

Food costs in Richmond were found to be higher than in the other boroughs and clothing costs lower in Brooklyn than elsewhere. Except for carfare, the cost of sundries was estimated at much the same figure everywhere, since these estimates are arbitrary, and, while a large body of data on these items were carefully collected and sifted there is the possibility that such cost differences as appeared were due to differences in samples rather than to intrinsic price differentials, and the probability that for the same quality of service the same prices would prevail.

On the other hand, what is obtained for a given outlay may be very different in the more suburban areas from what the same sum will buy in the city. Light, air, sunshine, quiet, green trees, proximity to beach and open country often compensate for a long train or subway ride and other inconveniences. Families which have become accustomed to the more rural areas seldom return to the city, while the exodus from the city proceeds at a steady rate. Brooklyn and Manhattan cannot provide the kind of living to be found in the less thickly settled boroughs and before long the Bronx also will be pretty thoroughly urbanized. Queens and

Richmond are, therefore, likely to be sought by those who for one reason or another require a more rural home. The cost, in any event will be much the same, except for carfares to town, which add somewhat to the cost of living at the specified standard, whatever that may be.

CHAPTER IX

COST OF LIVING FOR SINGLE PERSONS

MANY single young men and most single young women employed in offices in New York City and living at a minimum standard live at home as part of a family group. The cost of living for a single female industrial worker under these conditions was worked out in Chapter VII. The same method may be used for office workers. It is useful for comparative purposes, however, to estimate their cost of living when they are faced with the necessity of living among strangers. The young men who live in this way usually hire a room with one or more companions and eat in restaurants and cafeterias. The young women for the most part do this, also, although some of them get all or part of their meals at home. In Richmond, board and room are sometimes offered in the same house but this is not the usual arrangement.

Lodging

Furnished rooms rent for almost any sum the would-be occupant can pay. The problem of determining the minimum cost is one, then, of fixing the standard and pricing it. For a young unmarried woman, these standards have been fairly well established by the social agencies in the city concerned with housing girls, and include provision for cleanliness, privacy, heat and similar requirements. For young men, the same standards might be desirable although no one seems so interested in enforcing them. A surprising number of rooms are for rent in apartments where little or no privacy is assured and where being properly warmed seems likely to be a matter of chance.

The agencies consulted and rooms inspected in the present study indicate that for an office worker living in the Bronx, at least $6 a week would be necessary in the spring of 1926 to secure desirable accommodations; in Brooklyn, $5 was the apparent minimum; in Manhattan, rooms ranged from $4 up; $7 was the very least for which a satisfactory place could be secured. In Queens, likewise, $7 would be required to meet the demands of warmth, privacy and convenience. Room rents in Richmond vary from season to season, since accommodations are more in demand in the summer and less in the winter. An average minimum rate for a comfortable room the year round may be estimated at $5 weekly.

These amounts would pay for a variety of accommodations. It might be a small single room in a family where the type of lodger is more important than the rent; it might be for part of a double room with a private family or in a lodging house; it might, in a few instances, provide light housekeeping privileges or the share of room rent when board was furnished in conjunction therewith. In any case, however, not less than the sums here allowed would suffice for an average minimum of the outlay necessary for lodging for office workers living at a fair American standard in New York in the spring of 1926.[1]

Food

Young men and young women living in furnished rooms generally eat their meals out. The estimate previously given of $1.25 a day as necessary for food for young male industrial workers may also be adopted for young male office employees, since, as pointed out when discussing relative food values for families of these occupational classes, those at sedentary occupations eat somewhat lighter foods containing less energy than those at heavier work who

[1] There are in the city a number of so-called homes, hotels, apartments and clubs organized specifically to provide suitable living accommodations for young girls with small incomes. In Manhattan alone there are 64 such houses accommodating 5,558 guests, and while the other boroughs do not provide anything like a similar number of accommodations, they are perhaps in proportion to their needs. Almost all of these houses are subsidized in some way, so that the young women living in them do not pay their complete cost of living. Rates range from $4.50 to $14.50 a week for room and board. All of them have facilities for laundry and sewing, sometimes free, sometimes at a nominal fee. Since, however, the charges do not cover the full cost of support, the cost of living at these places has not been taken as representative. For young men, also, a few social welfare organizations provide rooms somewhat below the going rate for similar accommodations offered on a commercial basis.

require more energy and get it in a bulkier and less expensive form, but at substantially identical costs.

Assuming that a young girl was eating her meals in lunch rooms and cafeterias, the cost of food was at least one dollar a day in all boroughs in the spring of 1926. This figure is based on estimates from a cafeteria in Brooklyn that the average check at noon was 30 cents and at night, 40 cents; in one of the Manhattan cafeterias the average noon check was said to be 45 cents; in the Bronx, a similar cafeteria stated that the average woman's noon check was 30 or 40 cents. It is not known, of course, the extent to which the meal for which average expenditures are given represents the principal meal of the day, or how adequate the food secured for this outlay was, but one dollar a day apparently would provide for a light breakfast[1] and lunch, and sufficiently substantial dinner for a woman at office work, together with occasional extra fruit or crackers.[2] So far as can be determined from average restaurant prices, there is little difference in cost at comparable eating places in the five boroughs. In Richmond, where food might be expected to be slightly higher because of the somewhat greater cost of raw materials, the custom of paying a flat rate for board and room brought the average down to the level of the other boroughs.

In those cases where several young women lived together and cooked their own meals, the average minimum cost of food was probably about half that which they would have to pay when it was eaten in a restaurant. Four dollars a week would seem to be an ample minimum allowance.[3] In this case, however, their rooms, with conveniences for cooking, would often cost more than the amounts mentioned earlier for the lodging item.

[1] It is a fairly common practice for girls to be allowed to get their breakfast in the house where they room, even though no other meals are prepared there.

[2] This is lower than the estimate by one organization in Manhattan, that $10.50 a week would be necessary to feed a girl eating all of her meals at a restaurant. The latter seems high, especially in view of the fact that many of the large business organizations, employing thousands of young women workers, supply a hearty meal at noon practically at cost.

[3] See Table 4. One of the social organizations concerned with proper housing for girls estimated that girls who did their own cooking could live well on $4 a week; another placed this estimate at $5.

TABLE 24: AVERAGE MINIMUM COST OF CLOTHING FOR ONE YEAR FOR A SINGLE FEMALE OFFICE WORKER LIVING AT A FAIR AMERICAN STANDARD IN NEW YORK CITY, 1926

(National Industrial Conference Board)

Item	Quantity Allowance	Bronx		Brooklyn		Manhattan		Queens		Richmond	
		Average Price	Yearly Cost	Average Price	Yearly Cost	Average Price	Yearly Cost	Average Price	Yearly Cost	Average Price	Yearly Cost
Coat	1	$13.06	$13.06	$10.50	$10.50	$14.90	$14.90	$13.67	$13.67	$11.25	$11.25
Suit	½	14.83	7.42	16.21	8.11	15.35	7.68	18.57	9.29	19.75	9.88
Sweater	½	3.15	1.58	2.30	1.15	3.30	1.65	3.68	1.84	2.32	1.16
Wool dress	1	10.01	10.01	5.83	5.83	6.29	6.29	8.12	8.12	7.50	7.50
Silk dress	1	9.98	9.98	7.14	7.14	8.32	8.32	8.84	8.84	9.61	9.61
Cotton dress	2	2.14	4.28	1.89	3.78	2.79	5.58	2.13	4.26	2.03	4.06
Silk overblouse	1	4.40	4.40	3.30	3.30	4.04	4.04	4.09	4.09	3.87	3.87
Cotton overblouse	2	1.51	3.02	1.21	2.42	1.35	2.70	1.53	3.06	1.32	2.64
Wool stockings	2	.80	1.60	.69	1.38	.86	1.72	.83	1.66	.76	1.52
Silk stockings	4	1.01	4.04	.83	3.32	1.04	4.16	.70	2.80	.87	3.48
Muslin nightgown	1	1.03	1.03	.81	.81	1.05	1.05	.91	.91	.90	.90
Outing flannel nightgown	1	1.06	1.06	.88	.88	1.03	1.03	.97	.97	.99	.99
Corset	1	1.23	1.23	1.11	1.11	1.80	1.80	1.22	1.22	1.15	1.15
Brassiere	2	.46	.92	.44	.88	.58	1.16	.45	.90	.46	.92
Cotton vest	2	.32	.64	.31	.62	.31	.62	.27	.54	.29	.58
Cotton bloomers	3	.61	1.83	.54	1.62	.54	1.62	.55	1.65	.54	1.62
Winter union suit	2	1.10	2.20	.85	1.70	1.19	2.38	1.09	2.18	1.18	2.36
Sateen dress slip	1	1.04	1.04	1.11	1.11	1.32	1.32	1.02	1.02	1.04	1.04
Cotton crepe kimono	⅓	1.04	.35	1.46	.49	1.61	.54	1.71	.57	1.72	.57
Summer hat	2	3.77	7.54	1.91	3.82	2.96	5.92	2.31	4.62	2.74	5.48
Winter hat	1	2.73	2.73	1.91	1.91	2.91	2.91	2.31	2.31	2.74	2.74
Chamoisette gloves	2	.86	1.72	.63	1.26	.79	1.58	.79	1.58	.84	1.68
Felt house slippers	⅓	.78	.26	.74	.25	.77	.26	.77	.26	.82	.27
Oxfords	1½	4.22	6.33	3.98	5.97	4.75	7.13	4.04	6.06	3.26	4.89
Pumps	1	4.19	4.19	3.98	3.98	4.67	4.67	4.10	4.10	3.26	3.26
Rubbers	1	1.14	1.14	1.07	1.07	1.05	1.05	1.05	1.05	.96	.96
Umbrella	½	1.00	.50	.98	.49	1.25	.63	1.09	.55	1.25	.63
Handkerchief	8	.08	.64	.06	.48	.10	.80	.08	.64	.10	.80
Handbag	1	1.56	1.56	.80	.80	1.50	1.50	.90	.90	1.00	1.00
Cleaning and pressing	2	1.70	3.40	2.17	4.34	1.63	3.26	1.92	3.84	2.00	4.00
Half-soles and heels	2	1.44	2.88	1.25	2.50	1.31	2.62	1.25	2.50	1.50	3.00
Heels	2	.46	.92	.50	1.00	.44	.88	.50	1.00	.50	1.00
Incidentals			5.00		5.00		5.00		5.00		5.00
Total			$108.50		$89.02		$106.77		$102.00		$99.81

Clothing

As already noted in discussing the clothing requirements of an unmarried male industrial worker, a man who does not have in his family some one to attend to the minor repairs in his clothing must pay to have this work done, or, failing to have the stitches taken in time, must replace his garments more frequently than does a man whose clothing is cleaned and mended as occasion requires. To take account of this circumstance, 30% has been added to the clothing allowance for the married office worker to provide for the requirements of an unmarried man in a similar occupation.

The clothing budget for a young woman office worker, based on prices in the spring of 1926, is given in Table 24. This was made up on the assumption that she bought all of her clothing ready to wear, and that she was required to maintain a neat appearance at her work. The custom of wearing smocks in many of the New York offices was not taken into account, and that, by lessening the wear on dresses or making possible the wearing of older garments beneath them, might reduce the cost of clothing somewhat. It is likely, also, that many office workers are employed in localities where there are shops catering especially to their trade and where unusual values may at times be had at sales. If the young woman made some of her own dresses, the cost of her clothing would be still further reduced below the amounts allowed, based on the purchase of everything ready to wear.

Sundries

The sundries items cost for single men and single women office employees, living apart from a family group, as shown in Table 25 and Table 26 were derived from data presented in Chapter V and follow the same general theories as those on which the estimates in Table 14 and Table 16 were predicated. The allowances assume the necessity for providing not only for obvious needs but they also assume that a certain amount of recreation and association with one's kind is required, that medical attention should be paid for, that reading the daily paper, writing letters and telephoning are the prerogatives of American citizens, that self-respecting

TABLE 25: AVERAGE MINIMUM COST OF MAINTAINING A FAIR AMERICAN STANDARD OF LIVING FOR A SINGLE MALE OFFICE WORKER LIVING APART FROM A FAMILY GROUP IN NEW YORK CITY, 1926

(National Industrial Conference Board)

Item	Bronx	Brooklyn	Manhattan	Queens	Richmond
Yearly Cost[a]					
Lodging	$312.00	$260.00	$364.00	$364.00	$260.00
Food	455.00	455.00	455.00	455.00	455.00
Clothing	103.87	102.47	104.04	101.84	94.54
Sundries					
Transportation	41.60	41.60	41.60	62.40	131.04[b]
Recreation	20.80	20.80	20.80	20.80	20.80
Reading material, stationery, postage, telephone, etc.	18.20	18.20	18.20	18.20	18.20
Medical care and sick benefits	20.80	20.80	20.80	20.80	20.80
Insurance	39.00	39.00	39.00	39.00	39.00
Organizations	13.00	13.00	13.00	13.00	13.00
Church, charity, gifts	10.40	10.40	10.40	10.40	10.40
Tobacco, candy, etc.	15.60	15.60	15.60	15.60	15.60
Toilet articles, hair cuts, etc.	20.80	20.80	20.80	20.80	20.80
Laundry	59.80	59.80	59.80	59.80	59.80
Total	$1,130.87	$1,077.47	$1,183.04	$1,201.64	$1,158.98[b]
Weekly Cost[a]					
Lodging	$6.00	$5.00	$7.00	$7.00	$5.00
Food	8.75	8.75	8.75	8.75	8.75
Clothing	2.00	1.97	2.00	1.96	1.82
Sundries					
Transportation	.80	.80	.80	1.20	2.52[b]
Recreation	.40	.40	.40	.40	.40
Reading material, stationery, postage, telephone, etc.	.35	.35	.35	.35	.35
Medical care and sick benefits	.40	.40	.40	.40	.40
Insurance	.75	.75	.75	.75	.75
Organizations	.25	.25	.25	.25	.25
Church, charity, gifts	.20	.20	.20	.20	.20
Tobacco, candy, etc.	.30	.30	.30	.30	.30
Toilet articles, hair cuts, etc.	.40	.40	.40	.40	.40
Laundry	1.15	1.15	1.15	1.15	1.15
Total	$21.75	$20.72	$22.75	$23.11	$22.29[b]

[a] The weekly cost of clothing was derived from the yearly; for all other items, the yearly cost was derived from the weekly. There is, therefore, a very slight discrepancy between the yearly and the weekly totals for the cost of living as a whole.

[b] Includes transportation to work in other boroughs.

TABLE 26: AVERAGE MINIMUM COST OF MAINTAINING A FAIR AMERICAN STANDARD OF LIVING FOR A SINGLE FEMALE OFFICE WORKER LIVING APART FROM A FAMILY GROUP IN NEW YORK CITY, 1926

(National Industrial Conference Board)

Item	Bronx	Brooklyn	Manhattan	Queens	Richmond
Yearly Cost[a]					
Lodging	$312.00	$260.00	$364.00	$364.00	$260.00
Food	364.00	364.00	364.00	364.00	364.00
Clothing	108.50	89.02	106.77	102.00	99.81
Sundries					
Transportation	36.40	36.40	36.40	54.60	121.68[b]
Recreation	10.40	10.40	10.40	10.40	10.40
Reading material, stationery, postage, telephone, etc.	18.20	18.20	18.20	18.20	18.20
Medical care and sick benefits	20.80	20.80	20.80	20.80	20.80
Insurance	26.00	26.00	26.00	26.00	26.00
Organizations	13.00	13.00	13.00	13.00	13.00
Church, charity, gifts	10.40	10.40	10.40	10.40	10.40
Candy, etc.	7.80	7.80	7.80	7.80	7.80
Vacation	26.00	26.00	26.00	26.00	26.00
Toilet articles and services	20.80	20.80	20.80	20.80	20.80
Laundry	33.80	33.80	33.80	33.80	33.80
Total	$1,008.10	$936.62	$1,058.37	$1,071.80	$1,032.69[b]
Weekly Cost[a]					
Lodging	$6.00	$5.00	$7.00	$7.00	$5.00
Food	7.00	7.00	7.00	7.00	7.00
Clothing	2.09	1.71	2.05	1.96	1.92
Sundries					
Transportation	.70	.70	.70	1.05	2.34[b]
Recreation	.20	.20	.20	.20	.20
Reading material, stationery, postage, telephone, etc.	.35	.35	.35	.35	.35
Medical care and sick benefits	.40	.40	.40	.40	.40
Insurance	.50	.50	.50	.50	.50
Organizations	.25	.25	.25	.25	.25
Church, charity, gifts	.20	.20	.20	.20	.20
Candy, etc.	.15	.15	.15	.15	.15
Vacation	.50	.50	.50	.50	.50
Toilet articles and services	.40	.40	.40	.40	.40
Laundry	.65	.65	.65	.65	.65
Total	$19.39	$18.01	$20.35	$20.61	$19.86[b]

[a] The weekly cost of clothing was derived from the yearly; for all other items the yearly cost was derived from the weekly. There is, therefore, a very slight discrepancy between the yearly and the weekly totals for the cost of living as a whole.

[b] Includes transportation to work in other boroughs.

humans wish to do their share, small though it may be, in supporting their church and larger social movements, and, finally, that the youthful period of single responsibility is the time when provision must be made for the future, for the losses due to unemployment or for the unusual burdens which the carrying of even a small life insurance may temporarily help to lighten.

The Complete Budget

Young men and young women working in offices and paying commercial rates for board and lodging required less to live in Brooklyn than in the other boroughs of New York City, in the spring of 1926, as is seen from the summary of necessary expenses itemized in Table 25 and Table 26. The figures given are average minima for a fair American standard of living. Individuals will necessarily adjust and rearrange to suit their own needs. It is doubtful if the young unmarried man could save very much from the amounts allowed here as a representative minimum outlay, although his peculiar condition might make possible or require a somewhat different arrangement of expenditures. For example, a long illness might necessitate doing without recreation for a time, in order to pay doctors' bills, or he might be one of the fortunate few who got his lodging for less than the average and thus could pay more for other things.

For the young woman, a few savings might be effected, such as reducing her clothing cost through home dressmaking, doing her own laundry, and getting her meals for less than they cost in a restaurant. These economies are practised by business women in the city far above the minimum standard described here, when necessity arises, and if unusual demands press heavily on the young office worker, or if she wishes to readjust her budget to permit expenditures not itemized here, there is no reason why she should not do so, with no loss to her standards.

CHAPTER X

THE COST OF LIVING IN NEW YORK CITY

IN THE preceding chapters the goods and services entering into the maintenance of a fair American standard of living in New York City and their cost in the spring of 1926 have been discussed from the point of view of conditions in the separate boroughs. It was shown that while for some items the means available for realizing this standard are more or less identical in the different sections of the city, for others there is little or no possibility of finding comparable conditions. Food, clothing and sundries for the most part can be duplicated from borough to borough, but housing and the correlative fuel consumption often differ radically. For this reason, no attempt was made to bring the estimated costs of securing the separate items together into figures which would represent the city as a whole.

When all of the goods and services are combined into a complete budget, however, the cost of living for a given type of individual or family unit is so similar in different sections of the city that a single figure for each very fairly represents the city as a whole and, with few exceptions, could be taken as a fair measure of the cost of living in any one of the boroughs. Because of this essential similarity of each to the average, such contrasts as there are in the standard and cost of living in New York City are best brought out by comparing conditions in one borough with those in another as was done in the earlier chapters. The present chapter however combines into a single set of figures those previously given by boroughs for the complete budget and thus affords a final estimate for New York City as a whole.

Industrial Workers

For an industrial worker, these costs are summarized in Table 27. The estimated minimum cost of maintaining a fair American standard of living for the city as a whole has been found, for each unit, by weighting the cost in the separate boroughs as given in Tables 13, 14 and 16 by the estimated population in 1926, as shown on pages 2 and 3.[1] The resulting average for New York City as a whole is a very little lower per week than the average for the Bronx, Manhattan and Queens, and a very little higher than similar figures for Brooklyn and Richmond.[2]

TABLE 27: AVERAGE MINIMUM COST OF MAINTAINING A FAIR AMERICAN STANDARD OF LIVING FOR INDUSTRIAL WORKERS IN NEW YORK CITY, 1926

(National Industrial Conference Board)

Unit	Yearly [a]	Weekly [a]
Family of man, wife, one child	$1,375.44	$26.45
Family of man, wife, two children	1,685.14	32.41
Family of man, wife, three children	1,880.17	36.16
Single man, living apart from family group	971.87	18.69
Single woman living as part of family group	665.25	12.80

[a] Inasmuch as for some items the yearly cost was derived from the weekly, and for others, the weekly was derived from the yearly, there is a very slight discrepancy between the yearly and the weekly totals for all items combined.

OFFICE WORKERS

For the families of office workers and for single male and single female office employees, similar combinations of figures for the separate boroughs, weighted according to estimated population in 1926, result in estimates of the minimum cost of maintaining a fair American standard of living in New York City as given in Table 28. These figures show that for families and for single men the average minimum cost of living in the city as a whole is higher than in the Bronx or Brooklyn, but lower than in Manhattan, Queens and Richmond, when carfare to the other boroughs is considered. For single women, the average for the city is lower than for any borough except Brooklyn.

Attention should again be called to the fact that differences in the cost of living for industrial workers and their families and for office workers and their families are based on prevail-

[1] Weights based on estimated population in 1926 instead of on those gainfully employed in 1920 were used because of the shifting in population, and, presumably of those gainfully employed, between1920 and 1926.

[2] For single workers, it is lower than in Richmond, also.

TABLE 28: AVERAGE MINIMUM COST OF MAINTAINING A FAIR AMERICAN STANDARD OF LIVING FOR OFFICE WORKERS IN NEW YORK CITY, 1926

(National Industrial Conference Board)

Unit	Yearly [a]	Weekly [a]
Family of man, wife, one child	$1,539.49	$29,61
Family of man, wife, two children	1,903.17	36.60
Family of man, wife, three children	2,119.11	40.75
Single man, living apart from family group	1,137.01	21.87
Single woman, living apart from family group	1,005.81	19.34

[a] Inasmuch as for some items the yearly cost was derived from the weekly, and for others, the weekly was derived from the yearly, there is a very slight discrepancy between the yearly and the weekly totals for all items combined.

ing differences in the standards of living of the two groups, resulting not only from dissimilarities in the requirements of their occupations but also from variations in customary tastes and habits of consumption.

SUMMARY

This investigation was designed to show the minimum cost of maintaining a fair American standard of living in New York City. On the basis of data collected in representative neighborhoods in the five boroughs, estimates were made for families of industrial workers and for families of office workers; for single men and for single women in industrial and in office occupations. The data relate to conditions in the spring of 1926.

Summarized, these data show that the cost of living was practically identical in all boroughs.

For the families of industrial workers, there was a very slight financial advantage to be gained through living in Brooklyn, with Richmond, Queens, the Bronx and Manhattan a little higher, in the order named (page 87). The average for the city as a whole differed from the average for the separate boroughs by less than one dollar a week (pages 87, 126).

For the families of office workers, the cost of living in the Bronx was lowest, except for the larger groups, with Brooklyn only a few dollars higher per year, Manhattan and Queens next and Richmond highest of all, when transportation to the other boroughs is included (page 114). Except for Richmond, the average in the separate boroughs differed by less than one dollar a week from the average for the city as a whole (pages 114, 127).

Unmarried workers both in industry and in offices found Brooklyn the cheapest place in which to live, with costs in the other boroughs very similar (pages 92, 97, 122, 123).

Such differences in the cost of living as were found from one section of the city to another were caused by differences in the cost of a number of items entering into the total budget. Where rents were relatively low, the cost of gas, electricity and food might be high, as in Richmond. The high cost of transportation from outlying areas to work in the city proper also to some extent counterbalanced lower rents. Clothing costs were low in Brooklyn and Richmond, and in Brooklyn these low clothing costs combined with about average costs for other items, and lower rents for industrial housing, fixed the standing of Brooklyn in relation to the other boroughs. Low clothing costs in Richmond, however, did not counteract the higher cost of food, gas, electricity and transportation in that borough. For office workers in Brooklyn, low clothing costs helped to counterbalance the greater outlay necessary for rents, which were higher there than in some other sections.

It should always be borne in mind in analyzing these figures that they refer to the standard of living locally prevailing and the means available for its realization by American wage earners in the different areas surveyed in the spring of 1926. Coal, gas, electricity and a few other items cost much the same wherever they are sold but for the great bulk of necessities there are differences which make standardization impractical if not impossible. Not only do wage earners in Manhattan not live in frame houses or wage earners in Richmond in steam heated apartments, but the grade of meats, dairy products and vegetables in the food shops, and the style, character and quality of garments in the clothing stores all reflect the local demand. To the extent that uniform grades were being maintained these grades were priced; otherwise the goods most in local use were necessarily included. The results show what industrial workers and what office workers were actually required to spend to maintain a minimum American standard in the spring of 1926.

It should be emphasized, furthermore, that the rent estimates were based on the outlay necessarily made by a new tenant, not on the basis of what actually was being paid by tenants who had occupied the premises for some time. Old tenants are protected by law from rent increases, but new tenants almost always pay more rent in the place to which they move, than has been required of them for comparable accommodations while under legal protection. This is true for popular types of housing in all boroughs. For this reason the average person of small or moderate means frequently finds moving, even within his accustomed neighborhood, a considerable hardship.

Finally, it should be noted that the estimates of the average minimum cost of maintaining a fair American standard of living given in this report are based on prices and not on expenditures, and they are not in any way related to the income of any one individual. As pointed out several times in the present discussion, in most families in New York City there is more than one wage earner, and the support of the group comes from the family pocket book. The services in the home contributed by those not gainfully employed are paid for by those who are, more or less in proportion to the relative value of the services rendered.

www.ingramcontent.com/pod-product-compliance
Lightning Source LLC
LaVergne TN
LVHW021412110826
845150LV00007B/1891

* 9 7 8 1 4 2 5 5 1 1 8 8 3 *